Practical Skills in Rational Emotive Behaviour Therapy

Professor Windy Dryden
Goldsmiths' College, University of London

Other titles in this series

Preparing for Client Change in Rational Emotive Behaviour Therapy
Facilitating Client Change in Rational Emotive Behaviour Therapy

This book is for:

Mum, Dad and Wendy (JT)
Mum, Dad and Louise (WD)

Rational Emotive Behaviour Therapy: A Client's Guide

John Traverse and Windy Dryden

Whurr Publishers Ltd
London

© 1995 Whurr Publishers Ltd
Whurr Publishers Ltd
19b Compton Terrace, London N1 2UN, England

British Library Cataloguing in Publication Data
A catalogue record for this book is available from the
British Library.

ISBN 1-897635-08-7

Printed and bound in the UK by Athenaeum Press Ltd,
Gateshead, Tyne & Wear

Preface

This book is for people who are thinking about, or currently engaged in, rational emotive behaviour therapy to help them improve their lives. It will help them to understand their therapy and get the most out of it, as well as helping them to keep practising once therapy is over.

In short, it will help them to work with the therapist as part of a team, the goal of which is to help clients make changes in their lifestyles.

Therapy often involves homework assignments and this book will give clients a good idea of some common examples. The therapist will recommend homework assignments; they are a very important part of therapy.

John Traverse
Windy Dryden
March 1995

Contents

Chapter 1
Something is wrong

The obvious point for starting to make changes in your life is with the realisation that something is wrong. It is this realisation that brought you into therapy and it is the important first step. Often it is difficult, however, to see what it is that is wrong and your therapist will help you with this.

How do we know when there is something wrong? What is it that lets us know that changes would be advisable? In trying to answer this question we look at three things:

1. How we feel.
2. What we do.
3. An understanding of the situation that we are in.

These three aspects of life are all amenable to change. Of these three the first two are the most important because how we feel and how we act are under our own direct control and are therefore most within our own ability to change.

By contrast, when we think about situations that we are in, they fall, broadly speaking, into two types:

1. Those that we can change.
2. Those that we cannot change.

For example, if you are in an unhappy marriage or a job that you find stressful, you can try to get your partner or colleagues to change; if they refuse you can either leave or decide to tolerate the situation gracefully. On the other hand, if after an accident you are disabled, there will be nothing you or anyone else can do to get rid of the disability. Even in this case it is possible to change how you feel about your disability and how to act and cope with it, so that you can increase your happiness despite it.

Although it is, of course, possible to try to change situations, in general people have more power over their own feelings and behaviour than they do over the situations that meet them in their lives. Although it is quite unnecessary to resign oneself to the bad things that happen in life, and equally unnecessary to believe or accept that bad circumstances will never and can never change, it is wise to change your own feelings about situations and your own ways of coping with them before trying to tackle the situation itself.

It is usually more sensible to try to change bad situations only when you are coping as well as possible with the existing situation. In this way you become a better problem-solver, finding more acceptable solutions to your difficulties. When you learn to cope well with the bad events and to think about them rationally, you make them more tolerable to yourself, on the one hand, and you give yourself a better chance to change the situation, on the other.

When you are faced with unchangeable bad conditions you can still change how you feel about them and how you cope with the difficulties that arise.

Problems with emotions and behaviours

Anxiety

One of the most common emotional problems is anxiety and the fear and worry that go with it. Anxiety is probably common because there are usually good biological reasons for it.

Anxiety developed during the evolution of human beings, as a way of helping to deal with immediate threats. It was useful for our ancestors because it increased their awareness of immediate physical danger and, as a result, increased their chance of survival in a world where obvious physical danger was ever present in the form, for example, of attack by predatory wild animals.

Anxiety caused a sudden and dramatic release of adrenaline which made the body better able to spring into action either to fight or to run away – this is the fight or flight response. By engaging in the appropriate physical action the body systems would then return to the normal state when the person had fought off or run away from the attacker.

Although our modern civilised society is not the same as our ancestors' world, we still have this physiological mechanism for dealing with danger, be it existing or anticipated. In the modern world, however, anxiety – or stress as it is often called – follows from more abstract things such as a fear of failing or a fear of disapproval.

In Chapter 3 the cause of these fears will be explained, but for now we will examine their effects.

The effects of anxiety

As we begin to think about our fears the anxiety response sends adrenaline into the system and we cannot work it off in the physical way that was used by our ancestors. When a lion is chasing someone he can fight it or run away, so it is helpful to feel afraid of a lion and to take some physical action.

By contrast, it is impossible physically to fight or run away from or 'avoid' a fear of failure or a fear of disapproval. We then begin to experience side effects of anxiety such as heart pounding, tingling sensations or numbness in our hands or feet; dizziness may come over us, and we may experience a strange feeling as if we are not really here. Our breathing pattern might change so that we gasp for breath or even begin to feel sick. This is a description of what is often described as a panic attack, which is a form of anxiety problem.

Although panic attacks or anxiety in general is not actually dangerous, not surprisingly people think about what they are experiencing and might then make themselves even more anxious about the anxiety. In other words they become anxious about feeling anxiety which, of course, only serves to increase the anxiety.

Worry and its relationship to anxiety

Another form of anxiety in a sense is worry. People who worry constantly think about and churn over in their minds examples of times when they felt anxious and times when they anticipated or expected to feel anxious. As with avoiding problems, this is not a helpful coping strategy because it makes the anxiety worse.

In more severe instances people worry to the extent that they cannot seem to get worry off their mind, and they worry compulsively, over the same thoughts again and again. Additionally, some people become quite obsessional in their behaviour, repeatedly checking things such as taps or the locks on doors, in an effort to make absolutely certain that they have not made a mistake.

Anxiety, then, can sometimes lead to obsessional behaviour and compulsive thinking. Very often people who feel anxious spend a lot of time worrying and avoiding things. If you recognise any of these difficulties in yourself you are probably experiencing anxiety, and you would be well advised to think about making changes in how you feel and how you cope.

Anger and losing your temper

Most people recognise these days that anxiety – or its other name, stress – is a very common problem in the world. There is another common emotional problem that people often seem less willing to recognise as a problem – anger and the hostility that goes with it.

Perhaps one of the reasons why people do not recognise anger as an emotional problem is because it often seems righteous or justifiable. As shown in Chapter 3, anger is not, in fact, justifiable in the strict sense of the word. However, even if for a moment we assume that it is, we can still show you why anger is a problem.

The consequences of losing your temper

Anger is a problem because of the consequences it has both for the person and for other people who come into contact with that person. Think about the last time you saw an angry person and you will soon see that the anger did not help improve the situation. In fact, feeling angry invariably makes things worse.

As Chapter 3 will make clear, this does not imply that you have to learn to turn the other cheek every time. There are other, healthier emotions to feel instead of anger which do not involve compromising your values or wishes.

When someone feels angry he usually copes by 'blowing his top' and losing his temper. Although some people say that letting it out is healthy and helpful, usually it is not. In fact, if you feel angry and lose your temper, the chances are that you will then have to deal with a person getting angry back at you, dismissing you and not taking you seriously, or responding with aggression and physical violence.

All these responses, of course, help you to wind yourself up into a cycle of increased anger and loss of temper. This is the kind of problem that leads to unpleasant dealings with the nation's legal system: it is the kind of thing that destroys trust, wrecks marriages and loses friendships.

Anger has other bad effects, too, on the angry person. Not only does it put paid to problem-solving and healthy coping responses, it also raises the person's blood pressure and, if it goes on for long enough, produces considerable physical ill-health.

Anger is, of course, something that we all feel from time to time. However, if you find yourself feeling angry and losing your temper a lot of the time, or if friends and loved ones say that you do this, or if you do not lose your temper very often but when you do you tend to get physically violent, then anger is an emotional problem for you and you would do well to consider making changes.

Depression

Another common emotional difficulty many people experience is depression. This is not the same as sadness or 'feeling blue' which is often quite a healthy emotion.

The person who is feeling depressed often sees him- or herself as helpless and the world as hopeless. Although still able to hold a conversation that person feels cut off from all the other people around, even caring people who genuinely seem to want to help. He or she often feels tearful at the slightest thing, wants to be alone all the time, finds it very hard to take pleasure in anything and may even think that suicide is the only way out of a pointless world.

If you experience any of the difficulties listed above you can be helped, and you can help yourself as well, so do not give up.

If you are thinking of suicide, remember that suicide is final; there is no way back for you or those you love. The thoughts of hopelessness and helplessness that can make suicide seem like an option are part of experiencing depression and, although you may feel that way now, there is nothing to say that you will feel that way forever.

If you are feeling that way right now go and see your family doctor; your therapist can also help with this painful, unhealthy emotion. A lot of research has shown that, although the feelings of despair and thoughts of hopelessness and helplessness that go with ideas of suicide are very painful, they do not last forever.

No matter how hard it seems at the time, happiness is always a possibility. Tragically, the person who takes his or her life ends the prospect of happiness forever.

Recognising that you are depressed

Many people, however, do not feel like ending their lives even though they are feeling depressed. In these instances it may not be easy to recognise whether they are depressed.

If you tend to feel anxious and angry a lot of the time, feel tired most of the time, weak and lacking in energy, have difficulty in sleeping and in concentrating, often wake up very early, and have little or no interest in sex, you would be wise to think about the possibility that you are depressed. If you have experienced many of these difficulties for a prolonged period of time you may be experiencing depression. If so, you can make some changes in how you feel and cope, but, if in doubt, once again consult your family doctor.

Another way to recognise that you feel depressed is to think about whether there have recently been any major changes in your life, such as the loss of a loved one, moving house, changes at work such as a new boss or new job roles, illness in the family or any other alterations in circumstances.

Some kinds of depression are partly biological

It is important to note that some forms of depression are caused by biological factors, and this could be important in the following circumstances:

1. You have been depressed for a long time.
2. You have a relative who suffered with depression.
3. You cannot identify any life changes that took place in the last year or two.

Once again, if you think that this may be so, help is at hand; you would do well to ask your family doctor for some advice.

When people have biological forms of depression, they often also have the psychological forms of the illness, so even if your depression is partly biological you can be helped – and you can be taught how to help yourself. You can change your feelings of depression and learn new ways of coping with it.

Depression and anger are sometimes linked

A final note about depression is that it can be hidden by anger; often someone who is angry is also depressed. Furthermore, someone who has been experiencing other emotional problems such as anxiety or anger can get quite depressed over other problems. For example, many people who spend years feeling anxious about meeting other people can then become depressed about feeling anxious. The cause of this will be explained in Chapter 3.

Guilt

Anxiety, anger and depression are common emotional problems that most people will experience at some time in their lives and which are generally recognised in society as being problematic feelings to have. There are other emotions that are just as common, but perhaps not talked or written about as much as the three emotions discussed so far.

One of these is guilt. Guilt is one of those emotions that we often keep to ourselves because of the other feelings that go with it. Having recognised this fact, probably everyone knows from personal experience what guilt feels like.

Guilt is often associated with fear and depression. The person who feels guilty is often afraid of being found out and/or often feels depressed as well. The idea that people can be 'racked with guilt' helps us to understand just how painful this emotion can be, and how important is it to try to make changes if you are feeling guilty.

It is important to note that people feel guilty if they think that they have broken a moral code, ethical principle or value, and then bring a 'dogmatic attitude' to this thought. Chapter 3 will describe the importance of 'dogmatic' attitudes in more detail.

Alternatively, guilt occurs when the person focuses on the consequences of what he did or did not do, especially when the consequence was that another person was hurt. These are both examples of 'episodic guilt' because they focus on guilt that is rooted in particular episodes or actions.

There is also a third form of guilt, called 'existential guilt', in which people have a particular dogmatic attitude towards themselves which is focused on who they are rather than on what they have done or not done in life. This type of guilt is enduring and does not relate to any particular episode or action.

The consequences of feeling guilty

In a way guilt is a bit like anger in the sense that some people say that guilt is righteous and healthy because it can motivate the person to try to put right a wrong or at least to apologise for it. It could, the argument goes, help people learn not to do it again.

If these ideas were true it would make sense to say that guilt is not an emotion that is a sensible target for this book. In other words, if a person feels guilty he or she should not try to make changes in that emotion. Obviously this line of argument follows from the idea that the consequences of guilt are positive or helpful in some way.

We argue that the consequences of 'constructive remorse' are helpful. Put another way, there are alternative feelings, as Chapter 3 will make clear, which recognise wrong-doing but which are more constructive and helpful than guilt.

The usual coping responses to guilty feelings are often fear, and then attempts to avoid the problem. In cases of severe guilt and self-blame the person often seeks to do him- or herself harm. Sometimes people who feel guilty will dislike themselves so much that they think of themselves as totally undeserving of any kind of pleasure or happiness, and then will feel depressed.

Another type of self-defeating coping style which is associated with guilty feeling is obsessional checking – an effort by the person to make absolutely sure that he has not done anything wrong, followed by compulsive worrying about the prospect either of doing wrong or of making mistakes. Obsessive–compulsive problems can therefore be related to guilt as well as to anxiety.

As with all the emotions discussed so far, guilt can rob a person of his ability to find other, more healthy, ways of coping and as such he feels guilty a lot of the time; if that person uses the self-defeating coping styles discussed above, once again he should consider making changes.

Relationship problems

Given that most of us spend most of the time living, working and socialising with other people, there is another set of emotions which we will consider. If you regularly experience any of these, you had better start thinking about making changes: jealousy and a difficulty with trusting other people which goes with it; shame; and embarrassment.

Jealousy

Jealousy and difficulty trusting people are not generally a problem with strangers. People tend to feel jealous of and find it difficult to trust either people they love and live with, or people with whom they have regular and frequent contact such as friends or workmates. Why suggest that these constitute emotional problems?

When people feel jealous they tend to cope with their feelings by: being unwilling to trust the person who is the object of their jealousy; demanding or insisting that this person never lets them down and shows them constant undying love and respect.

Jealousy often goes hand in hand with anger and depression; anger occurs if the object of the jealousy does let the person down, and depression if the object of the jealousy shows any hint of wanting to spend time without the jealous person. In that sense jealousy is also linked with anxiety or fear of rejection. Long-standing and strong jealousy is therefore an emotion that damages relationships be they marital, friendship or work relationships.

The jealous person is often likely to find himself disadvantaged in his relationships, and even risks losing these relationships and experiencing a lonely life, spending a lot of time feeling hurt and anxious about either a real rejection or the prospect of a rejection. The person can run his life, on the one hand, trying to avoid rejection at all costs and, on the other, behaving in ways that are likely to bring about the rejection that he fears so much.

Shame and embarrassment

Although it is not, perhaps, so common to feel jealous with strangers, it is quite common to feel ashamed or embarrassed with strangers as well as with people with whom we have close relationships.

For example, very many people feel intensely embarrassed at social gatherings: they hate parties, dread going and dread being invited. The slightest social gaff, or even the anticipation of making a mistake, fills them with embarrassment. Consequently, if they ever do go to parties they sit quietly by themselves, concentrating hard on not making a mistake or looking foolish. They find it hard to think of anything to say and find it equally hard to make acquaintances and friendships.

If they feel highly anxious it is probable that they will quickly avoid going to social events, turn down invitations and pretty soon life is likely to become a fairly lonely affair. Once again, if you recognise this pattern in yourself, you would be advised to make some change in your feelings and behaviour.

Self-defeating behaviours

So far in this chapter the main kinds of emotional problems and the self-defeating behavioural coping strategies or 'action tendencies' which are associated with them have been described. It has been suggested that they are all good grounds upon which to make a decision that it is time to make some changes in your feelings and behaviours.

The rest of this chapter will consider some other typical strategies which ultimately make matters worse and are therefore 'self-defeating'. Recognising that you use these strategies can help you to consider making changes in your ways of coping with difficulties.

The problem of the quick fix

The first of these problem strategies is 'the quick fix'. We live in a modern consumerist 'quick fix' society in which there is supposedly 'a pill for every ill'. A quick fix is any activity that a person does to overcome a feeling of discomfort or to obtain a feeling of comfort or euphoria.

The type of quick fix depends very much on the individual concerned, but a very common form of quick fix in our society is over-eating; for example, many people engage in 'comfort' eating in an attempt to avoid uncomfortable feelings such as boredom or depression. The disadvantages and danger of over-eating are well known and will not be documented here.

Another form of quick fix was the use of tranquillisers to overcome anxiety. Although tranquillisers can be a helpful short-term way of reducing the uncomfortable feeling of anxiety, it is not possible to make changes in that unpleasant emotion by taking tablets.

Almost anything can become a quick fix for avoiding discomfort and gaining comfort, such as chocolate or even shopping.

All quick fixes work in the short term because they have two things in common:

1. They help the user to avoid an uncomfortable state such as boredom.
2. They help to create a pleasurable state such as elation for a temporary period.

The thing that makes something a quick fix is not the thing itself but the motivation behind its use. Quick fixes, because they act quickly, can become addictions which create a new set of difficulties. The person thinks of the quick fix as the solution to this problem when, in fact, it is really only a way of hiding from or covering up a problem that the person thinks he cannot cope with.

When people do not get something they want they experience discomfort as a result. This discomfort is not in the mind, it is real. The painful negative feelings that result follow from the recognition that you are not getting something you wanted and value.

This is, of course, undesirable and bad, but problems arise when people convince themselves that it is more than bad, that it is terrible, and that they absolutely cannot stand the discomfort they feel. This is the route to taking quick fixes as a short-term temporary solution to problems.

However, as a coping strategy it tends not to work because the person hides from or avoids the real problem and gets used to acting in ways that bring about other problems.

All the major addictions we hear about and/or get stuck with ourselves, such as alcohol, drugs and gambling, have a large measure of the quick fix about them. Of these, probably the most common is alcohol addiction, probably because alcohol is so readily available.

The quick fix strategy seen in the examples given above often goes hand-in-hand with the types of problems described earlier in the chapter, such as anxiety and avoidance, anger and temper, etc. In addiction, however, when people are suffering from anxiety, depression, guilt or any other of these emotional troubles, it is very common to find that they want a quick fix for their emotional problems. Their requirement for a quick fix for their feelings of emotional discomfort makes it difficult for them to overcome their emotional problems.

If you show the kind of behaviour that is typical of the quick fix, on a regular basis, then recognise that this is not the long-term solution to your problem and consider making changes in this coping strategy.

Procrastination

The final self-defeating coping strategy to be discussed in this chapter is procrastination; this involves putting things off until you are faced with an enormous mess to deal with. In a sense procrastination is a form of avoidance; the person who is procrastinating avoids doing the things that it would be better to do.

Obviously we all put things off some of the time, but if you regularly put off lots of things, or if there is a special job or project that you would really like to get done but keep putting off, then you have a self-defeating coping strategy and some changes would be helpful for you.

Conclusion

By now you have a good idea of the kinds of emotional and behavioural problems that commonly afflict humankind. As people are very rich and complex, it is usual to find that people have more than one of the problems discussed in this chapter. It is very unusual to find, for example, that someone has a problem with anger alone and nothing else.

Typically, most humans have multiple problems, for example, with anger, guilt and the quick fix. So do not be surprised if you find that you, too, can see several areas of difficulty. Although these problems are very common, everyday occurrences, they are also painful, unpleasant and unnecessary.

That's right, they are not absolutely inevitable! You can do something about them. If you recognise any of these difficulties in your own life you can learn how to go about making changes in how you feel and in what you do that currently gives you pain or makes your problems worse. That is what this book is about.

At the end of this chapter, there is an Appendix with a list of problems that are common for many people. Pick four or five that you, personally, think apply to you and that you would like to change.

If you want to learn more about the problems discussed in this chapter, there are several excellent books, all published by Sheldon Press, which we recommend:

- Dryden W, Gordon J (1990) *Think Your Way to Happiness*.
- Dryden W, Gordon J (1993) *Beating the Comfort Trap*.
- Dryden W, Gordon J (1991) *How to Untangle Your Emotional Knots*.
- Dryden W (1994) *Overcoming Guilt*.
- Hauck P (1974) *Depression*.
- Hauck P (1980) *Calm Down*.

Your therapist will probably be willing to recommend other things to read which will be a helpful part of your therapy and of making changes.

The problems noted in this chapter are not the only ones that you can be helped with; they are just examples of some common ones. Please discuss with your therapist any other areas of your life in which you want some help.

Your therapist may sometimes make suggestions that she or he thinks you could consider working on. Remember, your therapist is there to help, and unless you disclose your problems it will be difficult to be helped to maximal effect. There is probably nothing that you could tell your therapist he or she has not heard before or, indeed, experienced him- or herself!

Appendix: problem checklist

Please place a tick or cross at the problem that applies to you:

- Feeling anxious or worried about making mistakes   [ ]
- Feeling anxious or worried about illness or physical symptoms [ ]
- Feeling anxious or worried about relationships   [ ]
- Feeling anxious or worried about work   [ ]
- Feeling anxious or worried about being unemployed   [ ]
- Feeling anxious or worried about sexuality   [ ]
- Feeling anxious or worried about money troubles   [ ]
- Feeling ashamed or embarrassed   [ ]
- Feeling angry   [ ]
- Difficult to control temper   [ ]
- Feeling anxious or worried about children   [ ]
- Getting jealous   [ ]
- Thinking I'm stupid/a failure/no good   [ ]
- Avoiding people, places or situations   [ ]
- Feeling very low or depressed   [ ]
- Thinking life is hopeless   [ ]
- Feeling guilty   [ ]
- Feeling lonely, difficult to make friends   [ ]
- Can't seem to make my mind up   [ ]
- Problem with eating   [ ]
- Want to lose weight but find it hard   [ ]
- Problem with drinking   [ ]
- Hard to cope with rejection   [ ]
- Afraid I might lose someone I love   [ ]
- Finding it hard to get rid of a bad habit   [ ]
- Hard to stop doing certain things   [ ]
- Hard to get certain thoughts off my mind   [ ]
- Being too careful with things   [ ]
- Thinking someone disapproves of me   [ ]
- Find it hard to say 'No' to people   [ ]
- Find it hard to ask people to help me out   [ ]
- Feeling bored or having nothing to do   [ ]
- Thinking about being badly treated   [ ]

Chapter 2
Commitment to change: the four major insights

Changing how we feel and how we behave is not easy. However, if you are going through some of the difficulties discussed in Chapter 1, then you are in emotional pain and you are probably sometimes doing things that make you your own worst enemy.

Ask yourself: 'Which is harder, making changes or staying the way I am?'

If you think about this carefully we think that you will realise that the old saying 'no pain, no gain' is probably true. Although you will probably not have to go through pain you will have to go through hard work and maybe some discomfort.

Sometimes you may not really want to go to your therapy session; we understand this and can help. But your efforts will be worth it in the end. Commit yourself now to making a better, happier life for yourself.

This book will teach you some powerful ideas and methods to help you change. Over the last 20 or 30 years, they have been used successfully by a large number of British and American psychologists to help many people.

These methods form an approach to psychotherapy called rational emotive behaviour therapy (REBT). Many people have helped themselves with REBT by reading books such as this one, by having therapy and by putting the ideas into practice.

Reading this book will give you a 'head start' to therapy and help therapy to progress more quickly and effectively.

REBT recognises how important it is to commit yourself to change and teaches four major ideas or 'insights' which are very important in the change process. These insights are important not just in getting started but to carrying through your efforts.

Insight 1: you largely make yourself psychologically disturbed

The first of the main ideas is very good news for you. Your current difficulties are not caused by your childhood. No matter how difficult, how painful or unpleasant your childhood was, such difficulties did not cause your current emotional and behavioural problems.

This is not to say that childhood is not important; of course it is. But if childhood problems caused problems in adulthood then every adult who had a reasonably happy childhood would be problem free and every adult who had an unhappy childhood would have an adulthood full of misery.

This is clearly not the case.

Furthermore, other people do not cause your current problems. They may contribute to your problems, but they do not cause them.

Why is this good news? It is good news because, unless you have a time machine, you cannot go back and change your childhood; therefore if your childhood was causing your problems then you would be stuck with them and change would be impossible. Fortunately, this is not the case.

Second, it is good news because, if other people caused your problems, to change them you would have to be a dictator who could make or force everyone else to do exactly what you want, when you want. Sometimes, of course, everyone may have a sneaking notion that this would be nice, but it is not the case; you are not a dictator. In any case, history tells us that dictators often come to sticky ends!

If these things are not creating your problems what is? The answer is: you are!

You produce your own emotional and behavioural problems. Situations obviously contribute to the problems that you have, but you are largely responsible for how you feel and what you do.

This is insight 1 and is the principle of 'emotional responsibility'. It is very important for making changes. Unless you accept this idea you will be unlikely to take responsibility for your own development and therefore you will be unlikely to change. Looking around for someone or something else to blame is, in a sense, comforting, but in the long run this strategy will imprison you in your own troubles just as surely as iron bars.

How you feel and behave is largely determined by the way you think, not by the things that happen to you or by the actions of other people. Chapter 3 provides much more detail about this idea, but for now the main point is the importance of this insight.

This is tremendously good news, because you can, if you accept this insight, learn to put yourself back in control of your feelings and actions.

You can learn to take control of your own life and of the changes you want to make.

Insight 2: you disturb yourself by holding a set of irrational beliefs

Regardless of what happened in the past – whether your parents loved you or not, whether you had a good deal or a raw deal – you first became emotionally disturbed when you adopted or agreed with certain unhealthy habits of thinking. As you will see in Chapter 3, these habits are very important to your own efforts to make changes and are called *irrational beliefs*. They are largely responsible for your psychological problems.

No matter how badly you were treated, you became emotionally disturbed and began to use self-defeating coping tactics when you agreed with these unhealthy thinking habits or irrational beliefs. It may be, indeed it is even likely, that significant people in your life also had some irrational beliefs of their own, and that they worked hard, often unintentionally, to teach them to you.

Even so, the problems began when you agreed with or accepted these unhealthy irrational beliefs.

It is for this reason that we can say that your past contributed to but did not cause your present problems. You get upset emotionally and behave in ways that make things worse for you because you keep practising and, in a sense, brain-washing yourself with the same irrational beliefs that you learned in the past.

As with insight 1, the second insight is good news because you can learn to root out and minimise these irrational beliefs; indeed, as you will see, this is the main powerhouse behind your efforts to make changes.

Insight 3: you can change

The first two insights stress the importance of accepting responsibility for your own problems and for your own changes. Insight 3 is equally important because, although you are largely responsible for creating and maintaining your own emotional and behavioural problems, insight 3 teaches you that it is important not to judge, blame or condemn yourself for having created and maintained the problems.

How can this be so? Surely if you are responsible you are also to blame! Not so. Read this insight very carefully, please.

As early as the 1960s Dr Albert Ellis realised that all human beings find it very easy to think irrationally and self-defeatingly. He argues that we come into the world with a strong ability to think irrationally. In other words, he noted that all human beings have a biological predisposition to think irrationally.

This does not say that characteristics cannot be changed. It simply means that because the tendency to think irrationally has a biological basis, an individual easily develops the habit of irrational thinking and has a difficult time changing this habit.

Dr Ellis amassed an impressive amount of evidence to support this important insight. Since then many more psychologists, psychiatrists and psychotherapists have found similar evidence.

Of course, it is only the tendency to think irrationally that has a biological basis. The human species is also a fantastic learning machine. People of all ages learn at an astonishing rate, and the content of any given individual's irrational beliefs is probably learned and self-taught. People therefore not only have the capacity to think irrationally, they can also learn to think rationally or in a healthy way.

This is insight 3. You, like every other human being, probably have an innate genetic tendency to think irrationally. So, if you ask the question 'Blast it, how can I be so stupid as to think irrationally?', the answer is because you are human. We can all think irrationally and, of course, we can also think rationally.

It is important to recognise your humanity: be gentle with yourself. Don't forget, you are not the first person to have problems and you will not be the last. The vast majority of human beings have the same problems you do. Forgive, and accept yourself, even though you created and maintained your problems. Then get round to working on making changes.

Insight 4: change involves commitment and effort

This insight follows partly from insight 3. Given a genetic tendency to think irrationally, people usually get a lot of unhealthy practice at thinking irrationally. By the time you read this you have probably done a good job of making your irrational beliefs 'second nature'; in other words, these habits of thinking are probably ingrained.

It is probable that you think and believe what you do without much conscious awareness and without pausing to question.

Therefore, it follows that a determined and sustained effort, first to make yourself aware of your irrational beliefs and second to change those beliefs, is necessary if you want to follow through on your commitment to making changes.

This is really where commitment becomes important. It is relatively easy to commit yourself to improving your life, to feeling and coping better. But when people realise that hard work and continual practice are necessary, they sometimes think again.

Unfortunately, there is no magic potion that can take the hard work and practice out of making changes, although no doubt the person who invents one will make a fortune! Until one comes along you are well advised to commit yourself to the hard work and practice that is part and parcel of making changes.

We think it will be worth it, and your therapist will show you how to put in the effort that is necessary for making changes, often recommending homework assignments that you can do outside the actual therapy sessions.

Chapter 3
The ABCs of rational emotive behaviour therapy

In any area of life, when we are beset by problems it is very difficult to be able to see the 'wood for the trees'. This is, of course, especially so when our problems are very personal and full of painful emotions.

Not surprisingly, people can easily become down-hearted and demoralised, and once this happens it is only too easy to give up and resign ourselves to the idea that it is too difficult to get over this, seemingly impossible, mess!

Understanding the ABCs

The ABCs of rational emotive behaviour therapy fulfil two very important roles. On the one hand, they help you to start to untangle the mess and to break it down into manageable proportions. In that sense the ABCs help you to avoid biting off more than you can chew.

The second important function is that the ABCs help you to operationalise the first two major insights into change that were described in Chapter 2. In other words, the ABCs help you to put the good ideals into actual practice.

This chapter will describe the ABCs of rational emotive behaviour therapy, or REBT, in more detail.

The money example

Imagine that you are about to go out and you do not know how much money you have got in your wallet or your purse. But you say, or think, to yourself: 'I'd like, I'd prefer, to have £10.00 on me but it isn't absolutely necessary.' You look in your pocket and find that you have got £9.00. How do you think you would feel?

The chances are that you would feel disappointed because you want £10.00 and have only got £9.00, but you probably would not feel angry or panicky.

This time, once again imagine that you are about to go out and you do not know how much money you have in your wallet or purse. But this time you think or say to yourself: 'I must have £10.00; I absolutely must have it.' You look in your pocket and find that you have got £9.00.

Now how do you think you will feel? This time you probably won't feel disappointed; you will feel something very different, probably panic or maybe anger! You would feel panic or anger because you believe you must have something and you have not got it.

A third example: imagine that you are about to go out and you do not know how much money you have in your purse or wallet. This time you say to yourself, 'I must have £10.00; I absolutely must have it.' You look in your wallet and find that you have got £11.00.

How do you think you will feel? Well, you will probably feel OK because you have got more than you are telling yourself you must have. But in about one minute you will think something that will make you feel panicky. Can you see what it is?

'But what if I lose £2.00; what if I spend £2.00; then I'll only have £9.00 and I must have £10.00!'

This story has three important points.

1. It illustrates the ABCs very well.
2. It teaches the difference between two kinds of beliefs.
3. It teaches us the difference between healthy and unhealthy negative emotions.

Illustration of the ABCs

'A' is a situation or event and in this case it is:

A – you go out of the house and you do not know how much money you have got.

'B' is a belief about 'A' and in this illustration there are two beliefs:

B1 – I'd like, or I'd prefer, to have £10.00 on me, but it isn't absolutely necersary.
B2 – I must have £10.00; I absolutely must have it.

'C' is a consequence which may be either an emotion or a behaviour. The consequence, and in this illustration the consequence is emotional, follows on or is determined by the belief at point B. In this case there were three emotional consequences:

C1 – disappointed
C2 – anxious (or angry)
C3 – panicky.

The exact nature of the emotion depends on the content or the words contained in the belief.

In a nutshell, this is the ABC:

A is a situation which triggers

B which is a belief, which is mainly responsible for

C which is an emotional or behavioural consequence of B.

The difference between two kinds of beliefs

This story teaches the difference between two kinds of beliefs. Rational beliefs are based on healthy preferences or desires. Irrational beliefs are based on unhealthy dogmatic demands.

If we retained healthy preferential or desiring beliefs we would not distress ourselves, but as you saw in Chapter 2 people have a strong tendency to think irrationally.

In other words, everybody has a strong tendency to take what we desire or prefer, and convince ourselves that we must have what we prefer. We can do this with tangible things such as money or a new car, but perhaps more importantly, human beings can do this with more intangible, abstract things, too, like love or approval or success!

When a situation A triggers an irrational belief – a demanding 'got to be' philosophy – it is our own self-created and highly practised demanding philosophy that leads to troublesome emotions and self-defeating coping strategies as a consequence of these beliefs at point C.

A demanding philosophy towards life will lead to problems when our demands are not met, but such a philosophy will also lead to problems when they are met, that is, because the demand will result in the kind of thinking that is typical of anxiety: 'What if I lose or I can't get the things I must have? What if my partner doesn't love me as he absolutely must!'

This is a typical irrational belief.

The difference between healthy and unhealthy negative emotions.

When you believe, 'I really want you to love me but you do not absolutely have to', and then we find out that the person, in fact, does not love us we will feel an appropriate healthy negative emotion, in this case probably sadness or disappointment. If the preference or desire is very strong, the emotional consequence will also be strong; in this case we would feel very disappointed or very sad.

However, when you believe, 'I really want you to love me: in fact, you absolutely have to because I desperately need you to love me', and then we find that, in fact, the person does not love us, now we feel a strong unhealthy negative emotion.

In fact, the irrational belief written at the start of this paragraph is an extremely common irrational belief. This leads to strong depression when we find we are not loved by the person whose love we convince ourselves we must have, and strong anxiety when we are loved because, of course, we might lose that love which we convince ourselves we absolutely need.

These are the main ideas behind the ABCs of REBT. The rest of the chapter will now explain these ideas in more detail and help you to begin to see how to use the ABCs to help yourself to make changes.

Putting the ABCs into practice

It is a fairly safe assumption that people do not want to change situations that are pleasant or enjoyable. There is, of course, no reason why they should want to change something that is to their own good. Problems, as stated in Chapter 1, concern situations that are bad, unpleasant or about which we feel some negative emotion.

What is it that defines a bad situation?

The place of goals in the ABCs

Every human being has goals that they aim towards, things that they would like to do or to have. However, a lot of the time most people are unclear about what their goals are at any given period in their lives. Their goals are often implicit and unstated, even to themselves.

A bad situation is one that conflicts with, or even gets in the way of, our goals. An important part of therapy is working out goals, and your therapist will spend time helping you to do that.

When in a bad situation we can then think rationally or irrationally about the fact that our goals are blocked.

If we think rationally we will feel a healthy negative emotion, but behave in a way that is likely to help us get back to our goal or find some other valued goal to replace it.

If we think irrationally, however, we will feel an unhealthy negative emotion and are likely to behave in a way that worsens the problem rather than improves it.

In its practical use, the ABC model starts with situations, or 'A's, in which our goal is blocked and the consequences, or 'C's, which follow from that. The purpose of using the ABCs is to work out the irrational beliefs that are producing the unhealthy emotions and self-defeating behaviours, and then change them to rational belief which will result in helpful feelings and constructive behaviour.

Summary of the ABCs

Figure 3.1 shows the process involved.

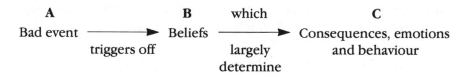

A   **B**   which   **C**
Bad event ──────▶ Beliefs ──────▶ Consequences, emotions
            triggers off   largely   and behaviour
                               determine

Figure 3.1

'A' can trigger either rational or irrational beliefs, which will determine
either helpful or unhelpful consequences, as shown in Figure 3.2:

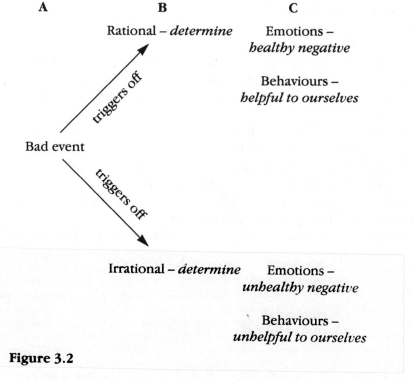

A   **B**   **C**

Rational – *determine*   Emotions –
                              healthy negative

                              Behaviours –
                              helpful to ourselves

Bad event

Irrational – *determine*   Emotions –
                              unhealthy negative

                              Behaviours –
                              unhelpful to ourselves

Figure 3.2

In making changes you have two jobs to do: first, recognise the irrational beliefs; second, change the irrational beliefs into rational ones.

When you accomplish this second task you will change the unhealthy
emotional and behavioural consequences to healthy motivating emotional
and behavioural consequences. Let us take an example from the list of
typical problems provided in Chapter 1.

Examples of ABCs in use

Let's take the example of feeling anxious or worried about work. Let's say that John's boss tells him that the company is going through a bad time and there are going to be some redundancies, but she does not know exactly who will lose their jobs. This counts as A.

A: Boss tells John there will be redundancies at work.
C: John feels anxious and makes more mistakes.

In this case we have both emotional and behavioural consequences.

Remember, the situation (or A) – John's boss telling him about redundancies – does not cause the consequences of him feeling anxious and making more mistakes. John creates those consequences mostly by his own irrational beliefs. The point of John using the ABCs is to *work out* what his irrational beliefs are and then *change them* to rational beliefs This is B in the ABC Framework.

Before we do that it is advisable for John to establish a goal – that is, what does he want to achieve.

The boss telling John of possible redundancies is a bad event because his goal is to have a reasonable job that he quite enjoys and earns money doing. Obviously, losing his job will block that goal. Therefore, this is a bad situation.

He may not be able to change the situation because he probably cannot force the company to do better or to keep him employed, but he can change his own emotional and behavioural consequences.

The question is, however, change them to what?

Would it be healthy for him to feel happy, or even calm, about the boss informing him of possible redundancies?

Certainly not; to achieve that goal he would have to try to fool himself into believing either that redundancy was good and valuable, or that there was absolutely nothing to worry about because it won't happen. It is very unlikely that this 'head in the sand' approach will help, and it certainly won't make the problem go away.

So what is the goal in this case? Will it help John to stay feeling anxious? Certainly not, but feeling happy is unrealistic.

A realistic feeling would be to feel concerned about the prospect of redundancy and emotionally this is his goal: to feel concerned. In addition, he might have a behavioural goal.

How about a behavioural goal of never making any mistakes at work? Is that a reasonable goal? Clearly it is not because everyone makes some mistakes; no one is perfect. So a better, more realistic goal is to reduce the number of mistakes he makes.

Here is the ABC with this problem so far:

A: Boss tells John that there will be redundancies at work.
iB:
C: Feel anxious.
           Make more mistakes.
Goal: Feel concerned.
           Reduce number of mistakes.

The next step is to work out what the irrational belief (iB) is that John has about being made redundant. The crucial step here is to ask what John is demanding must or must not happen?

In this case it is probable that John is believing something like:

iB: 'I absolutely must not be made redundant and I must have a guarantee that it will not happen.'

Given the situation A, this belief is bound to result in considerable anxiety and result in John making more mistakes at work. It is this irrational belief that is largely responsible for the unhealthy emotional and self-defeating behavioural consequences. Chapter 5 will teach you how to go about changing irrational beliefs.

Sometimes, use of this format makes it very easy to work out what any particular irrational belief is. Once you have identified the belief, then, and only then, are you in a position to change the belief into a rational belief.

However, sometimes, indeed perhaps usually, the belief that is causing the problem is not immediately obvious. If you practise using the ABCs you will get better and better at identifying your own irrational beliefs.

Remember insight 4, however: it takes hard work and practice – practise writing down the things that you want to change starting with the A or the C.

If you start with the A then write down how you feel about the A and/or how you behave at C.

If you start with the C then go back and write down the main point of the A, which is linked to the feeling and/or the behaviour.

When you are writing down the A try not to get bogged down in too much detail. Instead, just write down the main point of the situation.

Once you have got both the A and the C written down, then write down your goal: that is, write down a healthy feeling about the A and a helpful coping action. When you have done this, check that your goal is realistic.

You would be advised to practise doing this many times until it begins to be familiar to you. Do not expect it to be easy at first. You are learning a new skill, and like any new skill it takes practice and hard work. Your therapist will be very experienced in this process and will help you to learn to do it even when the problems facing you are very complex.

Meta-emotional problems

So far we have presented the ABCs as if they are simple and straightforward, and sometimes they are exactly that. However, humans being human they can also be more complicated: so what is it that complicates them?

Essentially, the main thing that complicates the ABCs is the fact that people quite often give themselves problems about their problems. For instance, they feel depressed about feeling anxious or guilty about losing their temper. These are called meta-emotions.

Let's go back to the example above and we will show you what we mean.

A: Boss tells John there will be redundancies at work.
iB: I absolutely must not be made redundant and must have a guarantee that it will not happen.
C: Feels anxious. Makes more mistakes.

If John gives himself a meta-emotional problem – and it may be, for example, depression – this is what happens:

The C I am feeling becomes a new A.

A: I feel anxious and I'm making mistakes.

This A then triggers a new irrational belief which creates a new C, in this case depression. Here the irrational belief would be something like:

iB: I should not feel anxious and I absolutely should not make so many mistakes.

This belief then creates the new:

C: Depression.

These secondary emotional problems are handled in just the same way as primary ABCs. In this case my goal would be to feel sad about feeling anxious and making more mistakes on the grounds that feeling anxious and making mistakes are themselves a bad event and that it would be unrealistic to feel happy about it.

In general, when you start to use the ABCs on a problem, two pieces of advice are relevant:

1. Stick with one problem at a time and don't jump about from one to another.

In general, when you start to use the ABCs on a problem, two pieces of advice are relevant:

1. Stick with one problem at a time and don't jump about from one to another.
2. As soon as you start on a problem take a moment or two to consider whether you give yourself two problems for the price of one.

If you do see that there is a secondary problem it is usually best to work on that one first, because if you do not do that the secondary problem will probably distract you from dealing with the primary problem.

The following are some common secondary problems:

1. Feeling ashamed about behaving shyly
2. Feeling depressed about feelings of anxiety
3. Feeling guilty about losing your temper
4. Feeling angry about feeling hurt
5. Over-eating to try to avoid feelings of depression
6. Feeling guilty and making yourself sick after binge eating
7. Feeling anxious about feelings of anxiety.

These are just a few examples and are by no means an exhaustive list.

This chapter has shown you how to understand the ABCs of REBT and how to put them into practice so as to be able to start the process of identifying your irrational beliefs. You might like to use the form below to help you to practise identifying the ABCs that you want to work on. This form will help you to identify 'A's, 'C's and secondary problems. We will help you to identify your irrational beliefs in Chapter 4.

Appendix: form 1 for practising ABCs

The problem I want to work on is:

A:

The feelings and behaviours that follow are:

C:
     My goal is to . . .
     feel . . .
     do . . .   and

Secondary problem:

When I feel . . . . . .
     or do . . . .
that is a new A.

When I feel or behave that way I
C: feel . . . . . .
     and do . . . . . .
My goal is to feel . . . . . .
     and do ...

Notice that this practice form does not yet contain the irrational beliefs that trigger the problem. This is for the following reasons:

1. The iBs are often difficult to identify. Chapter 4 contains some advice about how to identify the iBs.
2. The iBs themselves are usually more complex than has been shown so far. Chapter 4 will show you more about the nature of irrational beliefs.

Before you move on the Chapter 4 take a look at some examples of completed practice forms.

Example 1

The problem I want to work on is the following:

A: My partner never helps with the housework.

The feelings and behaviours that follow are:

C: **Feel**: I feel angry.

Do: I lose my temper and yell at him.

My goal is:

To feel: Irritated when he is lazy and
To do: Try to find a different way to persuade him rather than blow my
         top.

The secondary problem is:

When I feel angry and do lose my temper and yell at him, I:

C: **Feel**: Guilty
       Do: In this case it's really how I feel, I don't actually do anything.

My goal is to feel sorry for losing my temper but not guilty.

Example 2

The problem I want to work on is:

A: I can't seem to find a job.

The feelings and behaviours that follow are:

C: **Feel**: I feel depressed.
        Do: I do give up looking.

My goal is:

To feel: Sad that I can't find a job.
To do: Keep looking as hard as I can.

The secondary problem is:

When I feel depressed and do give up looking, I:

C: **Feel**: Angry.
        Do: Lose my temper in the Job Centre.

My goal is to feel irritated and to keep my temper in the Job Centre.

Example 3

The problem I want to work on is:

A: Whenever I meet people I stutter and stammer.

The feelings and behaviours that follow are:

C: **Feel**:   I feel anxious and sweat.
           Do: Avoid going to talk to people.

My goal is:

To feel: Concerned about meeting people
To do: Practise meeting and talking to people until I feel more
                  comfortable about doing that.

The secondary problem is:

We don't think that there is a secondary problem with this one.

Your therapist will guide you in the use of the ABC model in rational emotive behaviour therapy, but try to practise using it outside therapy. Then show your efforts to your therapist who will help you to resolve any difficulties you come up against.

Chapter 4
Identifying irrational beliefs

It can be quite difficult to work out what irrational beliefs are actually determining the emotional and behavioural difficulties that you want to change. As the overall point of the process is to change the irrational beliefs into rational beliefs, the step of identifying the irrational beliefs in the first place is obviously important.

If you practise and teach yourself to listen to your own irrational beliefs it will get easier.

This chapter is all about identifying irrational beliefs.

The ABCs of REBT are central to identifying irrational beliefs, and in this chapter you will find more information about 'A's, 'B's and 'C's. First, we will show you how to be fairly clear about what count as 'A's and what count as 'C's. Second, we will show you how to recognise an irrational belief when you see one.

More detail about the 'A's

When you think of describing an A – that is, a troublesome event in your life – think of it as containing two elements:

1. The actual events, that is, what actually happens
2. What you perceived or what you thought of it.

These two elements make up the A.

In trying to identify the irrational belief it is important to understand both what happened and what you thought about the actual event, because it is something in these two components that triggers the irrational beliefs.

The correct theoretical name for the A is the activating event, because it activated the irrational belief which, once it is activated, determines the unpleasant and unhealthy negative emotions and/or behavioural consequences. Understanding the A is one important way of identifying the irrational belief.

So, what is the difference between the actual event, that is, what happened, and the person's perception of, or thoughts about, the event?

Distinguishing between the 'event' and 'perception'

It will help to use an actual example. If I see a man walking down a street, that is an observation of an actual event. Most of the time I probably will not make anything of this event because it is irrelevant to me. More specifically, it has nothing to do with any of my interests in life or my goals.

If it has nothing to do with any of my interests or goals it is unlikely to have any emotional impact on me. Even so, I may perceive or think that the man is going to the post office. That is called an interpretation because the thought that he is going to the post office is a guess that goes beyond the event that I can actually observe.

So, seeing the man walking down the street is an actual event and the thought that he is going to the post office is an interpretation, or a guess, about the observed event. As the event and the interpretation about the event have nothing to do with any of my interests or goals, it is unlikely to activate any further beliefs.

Inferences trigger irrational beliefs

However, think about another example. I see a man walking down the street (event); I think that he is going to the bookshop to buy my birthday present (inference that goes beyond the observed event). This inference is relevant to my goals or interests because I like books. This issue of relevance defines the difference between an interpretation and an inference.

As it is relevant I then evaluate my inference: it is good that he is going to buy me a book because I like books and I like to receive gifts (this is an evaluative belief).

This evaluative belief is another term for 'B's, which evaluate or judge the inference. In this case the inference – he is going to the bookshop to buy my birthday present – triggered or activated a positive (and in this case) rational belief which then caused me a feeling of happiness.

This is one example of how:

A: event and inference
     activates or 'triggers'
B: belief
     which determines
C: emotional or behavioural consequences.

In this example, the entire ABC analysis is positive, but now we will show you a negative ABC example where an irrational belief is activated.

June sees her friend Jenny walking towards her; she walks past June and does not speak to her. This is an event because it is actually observable: it could be recorded on a video camera if we wanted to do that.

She then thinks, 'Jenny did not speak to me because she does not like me anymore'. This is an inference because it goes beyond what we can observe. Essentially she is guessing about the reason why Jenny did not speak to her. This is relevant to one of her goals, which is to have the person's friendship.

The inference now triggers, or activates, irrational belief: 'This is terrible. I need Jenny's friendship and I must get her to like me.' This belief is irrational because it is demanding or dogmatic – June is insisting that she must have Jenny's friendship.

This irrational belief then determines the emotional consequence that she feels depressed and the behavioural consequence that she begins to avoid her friend.

The ABC analysis is as follows:

A: **Event:** June's friend Jenny walks past her and does not speak to her.

Inference: Jenny did not speak to me because she does not like me any more.

This inference triggers B.

iB: Evaluation of the inference, that is, irrational belief.
This is terrible; I need Jenny's friendship; I must get her to like me.

This causes C.

C: **Emotional consequence:** Feels depressed.
Behavioural consequence: Begins to avoid Jenny.

It is important to notice that the inference that Jenny does not like June anymore does not, per se, cause the consequences, because that inference could trigger a different B. For instance, it could trigger the belief:

B: This does not matter because I never liked her anyway.

This belief would then not cause depression, but please note, this will only work if it is actually true; if you are lying to yourself, in other words you do like her, it will not work.

It could also trigger a healthy rational belief (rB) such as the following:

rB: This is bad because I would like to have Jenny's friendship but I do not need to have it. There is nothing to say; I must get her to like me, but of course I can try to get her to like me.

This rational belief would then elicit a different emotional consequence, probably disappointment, and a different behavioural consequence, probably asking Jenny what is wrong.

Let's take another example.

You ask your children to tidy up their room, but three days later it is still a mess. This is an event: we could video tape you asking them to tidy up and we could tape the untidied mess. It can be observed.

Then you think: my children do not respect me.

This is an inference: it goes beyond what we can observe. You are guessing about why they have not tidied up, and concluded that it is because they have no respect for you.

This inference now triggers an irrational belief: 'They absolutely should respect me; I'm their mother.' This belief is a dogmatic or demanding one, therefore it is irrational. This irrational belief then causes the emotional consequence that you feel angry, and the behavioural consequence that as soon as you get the chance you will scream at the kids and smack them.

Please note that in our experience of helping people change, this quite often leads to a secondary emotional problem, such as feeling guilty or depressed, but in this section we will not go into that possibility any further, so just please note it as a possibility for future reference.

In this case the ABC analysis is as follows:

A: **Event**:   You ask your children to tidy their room but three days later it is still a mess.
　　　Inference: My children do not respect me.

This inference triggers B.

iB: Evaluation of the inference, that is, irrational belief: They absolutely should respect me; I'm their mother.

This determines C.

C: Emotional consequences: You feel angry.
　　Behavioural consequences: You shout at them and smack them.

The event (the children not tidying up) and the inference (that they do not respect you) did not cause you to get angry and smack them. You created your anger and the loss of temper by your dogmatic demand that you absolutely must have the respect of your children.

A more healthy rational belief would state a healthy preference:

rB: I would very much like my children to respect me and do as I ask, but they do not absolutely have to.

With a very strong preference like this you would probably feel very annoyed if they don't respect you and would probably find a more helpful way of asserting your maternal or paternal preferences!

In identifying the irrational belief it is important to divide the A up into the actual event and the thoughts or inferences that you have about it. Of course, the event need not be in the past; it could be something you expect to happen.

Consider the following example: Peter is about to sit an examination in two weeks' time. This is an event: it has not happened yet, but when it does we can tape it with a video camera.

He thinks, 'I might fail this exam'. This is an inference because it goes beyond what we can observe. If he does fail then it will be an event, but until he fails it is an inference.

This activates the irrational belief: 'It will be terrible if I fail; I must pass.' This belief then causes Peter to feel anxious and to work so hard that he is not taking in the material that he wants to learn very well.

The ABCs are as follows:

A: **Event**:   Peter is going to sit an examination in two weeks.
          Inference: I might fail.

This triggers the irrational belief.

iB: Evaluation of the inference, that is, irrational belief: It will be terrible if I fail; I must pass.

This determines:

C: **Emotional consequences**:   Feels anxious.
          Behavioural consequences: Works so hard he doesn't learn
                                                           effectively.

In all the above examples the inference in each case could be correct or incorrect. In the first example it is quite possible that Jenny did not speak to June because she'd heard some bad news; in the second case, maybe the children just forgot; and in the third case Peter might not fail.

But that is not the point. It is also possible that the inference could be correct. It is not the inferences that do the emotional and/or behavioural damage, it is the irrational beliefs that you have about the inference. Or, in other words, how you evaluate the inference.

The inferences are likely to change as circumstances change, but your irrational beliefs are likely to be stable habits which do not change markedly unless, of course, you go out of your way purposely to change them.

Inference chaining

By identifying the inferences you make about the event you will be in a better position to identify the irrational belief because the belief is activated, or triggered, by the inference.

Sometimes the first inference you note down is the one that triggers the irrational belief, but more often inferences come in gangs or, more properly, 'chains'. Inferences are 'chained', or linked, together because one inference leads to another, which leads to another, and so on. We will show you what we mean.

In the early 1980s I (JT) studied in a big city and the route to college every morning took me through a very poor, rather run-down area with a lot of boarded-up shops and empty, vandalised houses. One morning as I drove through this area I began to feel anxious, and could not see why I felt that way. Once I took a look at my inferences and the irrational belief that was triggered by them, the root of my feeling of anxiety was clear.

It went like this:

A: Event: Driving into college through a run-down area, observing a
                 lot of closed shops and empty homes.
Inference 1: All these shops closed with people's hopes shattered.
Inference 2: I wonder where they are now. I bet there are a lot of
                 families and friendships broken up.
Inference 3: All that hard work just did not pay off for them.
Inference 4: What if all my hard work doesn't pay off?
Inference 5: What if I screw up and don't get my degree?

This triggers the irrational belief:

iB: I must not fail, I must get my degree. It will be a disaster if I don't.

This leads to:

C: **Emotional consequence**: I felt anxious.

Obviously this inference chain took a matter of milliseconds because people think very quickly. Also, because people are not used to thinking about their thinking it can seem a bit strange at first.

If you practise writing down, first of all, the actual event and then the inferences that follow, you will find that it is not all that difficult once you get used to it. Once you have got the inference chain written down on paper, take a look at all the inferences.

Which one is most closely related to the troublesome feeling or behaviour?

In the example above it was the final inference. But imagine instead that I had felt depressed not anxious. Looking back at the inference chain, inference 3 could be the one most closely related to feeling depressed. That inference could trigger the following irrational belief:

iB: It's terrible that hard work doesn't pay off. If you work hard you deserve to be happy and you absolutely should not have to suffer this way.

This leads to C:

C: **Emotional consequence**: depression.

When therapists see people to help them make changes, they often help them to work out their inference chains as a step towards identifying the irrational belief. To do this it is necessary first to work out the actual event and how they felt or what they did.

How to assess A

This involves making a note of what actually happened; this is the event. The actual event could be captured on film; it may involve what other people said or did, what you said or did, and what happened. In writing this chapter the event that you would see is the author sitting at a desk writing on a sheet of paper.

The event should be differentiated from any interpretation of it. An interpretation is your understanding of the event. The information that is necessary about the event is a description of it, not an interpretation.

An interpretation of the event that you see, namely the author writing in longhand, could be: 'The writer does not own a word processor.' Your interpretation could be correct or it could be wrong. Perhaps my word processor is currently broken.

Importantly, this interpretation is unlikely to lead to any emotion for you because you probably do not care one way or the other whether the author writes books with a pen or a computer, that is, your interpretation of the event is unimportant to you: it is not part of your 'personal domain'. Your personal domain covers events that are relevant and important in your life.

This is where inferences become relevant. Inferences are interpretations of events that are part of your own personal domain.

For example, suppose my (JT) father sees me writing those pages out on paper. He thinks, 'John has not got a word processor'. This is an interpretation not an inference because it is not important to him; he does not mind about me not having a word processor.

This interpretation then triggers the first link in an inference chain. My father's next inference might be: 'He will ask me to type up the manuscript'; this is part of his personal domain because it will take up his efforts and resources:

'He always wants everything done yesterday.'
'He will expect me to sit for hours at my computer when instead I want to watch the match.'
'He's always been a selfish sod.'

This final inference then triggers an irrational belief:

'He should not be so selfish'

which leads to the unhealthy feeling of anger.

In this example, both the final inference 'He's always been a selfish sod' and the irrational belief 'He should not be so selfish' contribute to the feeling of anger but, as noted in Chapter 3 in 'the money example', it is the irrational belief that largely determines the unhealthy emotion.

(Incidentally, JT's dad did type the manuscript . . . but willingly, we think!)

When you are assessing the A it is important to be clear about the actual event and then the inferences arising from it. The inferences are more important than the interpretations because the inferences are related to your 'personal domain', that is, they are closely associated with and trigger the irrational belief which largely determines the unhealthy feeling and self-defeating behaviours.

Once you have identified the inference that is most closely related to the unhealthy feeling, you will be in a good position to identify the irrational belief which is the main target for change.

Which is more important: the inference or the irrational belief?

The answer to this question is: both are important but the irrational belief is more important. This can be explained by an analogy.

Imagine that someone is pointing a gun at your head, but you and he know that the gun is empty. As the gun has no bullets, if he pulls the trigger all that will happen is that the gun makes a clicking sound. An empty gun cannot do you serious damage; even if he throws the gun at you, although unpleasant this would not kill or seriously hurt you.

Now imagine that someone has a handful of bullets but he does not have a gun. He could, of course, throw the bullets at you, but without a gun the bullets could not seriously hurt you; on their own they are not dangerous.

However, if someone points a loaded gun at your head and pulls the trigger, you will obviously be seriously hurt or even killed. Now, which did the damage: the bullet or the gun?

They both did: each on its own will not inflict much damage, but together they form a powerful team. The gun shoots (or triggers) the bullet which then makes a hole in your body; ultimately it is the bullet that results in the hole and in that sense, although both the gun and the bullet are important, the bullet is more important.

The inference is the gun in this analogy and the irrational belief is the bullet; they both do damage but it is the irrational belief that does the most damage.

The inference that is most closely linked to the unhealthy emotion 'triggers' or 'sets off' the irrational belief, which determines the unhealthy emotion. Your therapist will probably refer to that inference as the 'critical inference'.

In assessing the A, you and your therapist will often work out what the critical inference is that triggers your irrational belief for any given event. The event in question could be in the past or the present, or it could be an event that you anticipate in the future.

More information on 'inference chaining'

You will probably find that you and your therapist spend time working at the process of 'inference chaining'. This process is a way of identifying the critical inference that triggers the irrational belief.

I (WD) once had a client, Steve, who wanted therapy for the unhealthy emotion of anxiety. Here is an example of inference chaining with Steve. The event in consideration for Steve was his anticipation that he might fail his PhD examination. This is anticipatory or 'future-based' A.

Windy: OK, so let's see what you're anxious about. Imagine that you're sitting down and trying to work. Your mind is racing and you're fidgeting around. Now what do you think you would be anxious about?

Steve had already said that the event described above was typical whenever he tried to study for his examination.

Steve: I'd be anxious that my work would not be creative enough.
Windy: In whose opinion?
Steve: That's a good question. I think my supervisor's.
Windy: OK, let's assume for a moment that your supervisor would think your work wasn't creative enough.

Here Windy repeats Steve's inference (inference 1). This inference is relevant to Steve's personal domain in that it matters to him.

Windy: What would be anxiety provoking in your mind about that?

Here Windy asks Steve to think about the correlation, or link, between Steve's inference and his unhealthy emotion.

Steve: Well, it would remind me that I may not get my PhD.
Windy: That may or may not be true. People do get PhDs without showing that much creativity. But let's assume you're right and that you wouldn't get your PhD (inference 2). What would be anxiety provoking in your mind about that?

Windy asks Steve to comment on the link between inference 2 and the unhealthy emotion. Before doing this he points out that Steve's inference may not be true, but when doing inference chaining it is important to assume temporarily that the inference is true and this is what Windy does.

Steve: Well, I would not be able to get a top job in the city (inference 3).
Windy: Again, let's assume you are right. What would be anxiety provoking about not getting a job in the city?
Steve: Wait a minute, that's not the main thing. I guess it's the failure thing. I've never been able to contemplate failure and every time I focus on my work nowadays the thought that I might fail comes to mind (inference 4).
Windy: So, it's not so much your supervisor's opinion of your creativity or not getting a top job in the city. It's the thought of failing that you're most scared about, is that it?
Steve: Yeah, that's right.

In this example, using the technique of inference chaining, Steve and Windy have identified the critical inference 'I might fail my PhD', which triggers the irrational belief: 'I must not fail; if I do I would be a worthless failure.' This irrational belief then determines Steve's unhealthy emotion C, which is anxiety, and results in him putting off or avoiding getting down to studying.

In another example, I (JT) worked with a client, Jane, who wanted help with anger. The event was that Jane, who owed money to the bank from a failed business venture, had devised a scheme to repay the debt slowly. They rejected the plan and she felt angry.

John: The bank turned down your plan and you felt angry because…

Here John used a prompting question to help Jane make a link between her inferences and her unhealthy emotion.

Jane: Well, because they turned me down when I tried so hard (inference 1).

John: If you hadn't tried hard but they still turned you down would you have felt angry?

Jane: No.

John: What was anger provoking about having been turned down after trying so hard?

Jane: I was sure it would work after all that effort (inference 2) and it didn't.

John: OK, what was it about it not working that produced your anger?

Jane: Well, it's not fair (inference 3).

John: And what is it about that that ends up with you angry?

Jane: Well, it's just not fair!

John: I've written down your inferences. Take a look at them and tell me which one results in the most anger.

Jane: That one (points to inference 2).

They identified that the critical inference A 'I was sure it would work after all that effort and it didn't' triggered the irrational belief 'When I work hard at something it must work and if it doesn't I can't stand it', which determined her unhealthy emotion C: anger.

Importantly, she also held the irrational belief 'Life should always be fair', which also contributed to her anger.

More detail about the 'C's

It is not usually difficult to tell how you feel because the feelings that are determined by irrational beliefs are strong and painful. Even so, there can be some difficulties in working out how you are feeling and, until you can be clear to yourself about which particular feeling you want to work on, it is often difficult to identify the irrational belief that is creating this emotional problem.

This is often less of a problem when the goal is to change a behaviour such as losing your temper; you probably feel angry, and if you are very shy and avoid people you probably feel anxious. Working out what the behaviour is that you want to make changes in can help you to work out what emotion you want to change as well.

Do bear in mind that the C, the consequences does not have to be both an emotion and a behaviour – it could be one or the other.

One of the difficulties involved in working out the emotion can arise when there is a secondary problem, that you feel both angry and guilty. If you feel guilty about being angry, for instance, or about losing your temper, then it is probably best to begin by doing the ABCs on the guilty feeling and then move on to the anger after that.

Often, however, you can have more than one feeling about any given A. Take the example of driving into college described above. It is quite possible to feel both anxious and depressed, that is, because one inference triggers a belief that creates anxiety and another inference triggers a belief that results in depression.

In very complex situations, with lots of inferences all forming chains together and triggering several different irrational beliefs, it is quite possible to experience several emotions at once. When this happens it is advisable to work on one target C at a time, until you have worked through them all one by one.

If you try to do too many at once it's probable that you will get bogged down and confused, and then you are less likely to make changes in any of the problems.

When you have got a number of targets to attack don't get demoralised: Rome wasn't built in a day. If it takes more time it takes more time: simple as that.

Remember that identifying the C is a valuable step in helping you to identify the irrational belief.

The difference between healthy and unhealthy emotions

Another problem that often happens in identifying the C involves differentiating healthy negative emotions from unhealthy negative emotions.

Sometimes people misunderstand the difference between these two and try to change a healthy negative emotion. For example, JT has kept dogs all his life and becomes very attached to them. The breed of dog that he likes has a lifespan of between 10 and 12 years or so, and by now he has seen three or four very valued and loved pets die.

When this happens he feels very sad. In this case sadness is a healthy negative emotion and is determined by a rational belief; depression, however, is an unhealthy negative emotion and is created by an irrational belief.

If your employer tells you that the office where you work is going bankrupt and therefore you may be out of a job, you will feel very concerned. In this case a feeling of strong concern is a healthy negative emotion.

The former concern is determined by a rational belief about a negative event; the emotion of anxiety or panic is largely caused by an irrational belief about a negative event.

Sometimes people want, or expect, to have a positive feeling about a negative event. This is unrealistic and could only be achieved if you somehow fool yourself into thinking that a negative event is actually positive. Although it may well be possible to convince yourself that even a negative event had some good points, it's hard to see how you will convince yourself that a bad event is actually really a completely good event!

If anyone does manage to pull off this trick we hope that you will write and tell us how you did it!

The difference between healthy and unhealthy negative emotions depends upon the beliefs we have that lead to the emotions.

For example, concern is a healthy negative emotion which is associated with some threat such as loss of a job or ridicule. When a person feels concerned he or she would rationally believe: 'I hope this threat does not happen but there is nothing to say it must not happen. If it does happen it will be unfortunate.'

When a person feels anxious he or she would irrationally believe: 'This threat must not happen and it will be awful if it does.'

If we think irrationally about loss or failure we will feel depressed; but if we think rationally about loss or failure we will feel sad.

If we think irrationally about someone breaking one of our personal rules we will feel damning anger, but if we think rationally about someone breaking one of our personal rules we will feel non-damning anger (or irritation or annoyance, whichever word you prefer).

If we think irrationally about doing wrong or breaking our own moral code we will feel guilty, but if we think rationally about doing wrong or breaking our own moral code we will feel remorse or sorrow.

If we think irrationally about someone betraying us we will feel hurt, but if we think rationally about it we will feel disappointed.

If we think irrationally about a threat to a desired exclusive relationship we will feel irrational jealousy, but if we think rationally about it we will feel rational jealousy.

Finally, if we think irrationally about showing up a weakness in public or making a mistake in public we will feel shame or embarrassment, but if we think rationally about it we will feel regretful.

Table 4.1 shows a list of negative emotions: on the left are unhealthy negative emotions underpinned by irrational beliefs and on the right are healthy emotions determined by rational beliefs. The beliefs are all triggered by negative events. In general, we do not experience negative emotions about positive events.

The information provided above about the differences between healthy and unhealthy negative emotions can help you to work out which type of emotion you are feeling. When looking for a target C, examine the list of unhealthy emotions; these are all sensible targets for change.

Try to be clear about the words you use for your emotions. In our culture it is very common to use vague words like 'I felt bad'; ask your-

Table 4.1. Table of negative emotions

Unhealthy	Healthy
Anxiety	Concern
Depression	Sadness
Damning anger	Non-damning anger (or irritation or annoyance)
Guilt	Remorse or sorrow
Hurt	Disappointment
Irrational jealousy	Rational jealousy
Shame/Embarrassment	Regret

self what kind of 'bad' it was. If you felt 'upset' did you feel 'hurt upset' or 'angry, upset'?

If you are stuck check out what your inference is or ask yourself: 'If my best friend were in this situation what would he be feeling?' If in doubt take a wild guess: you'll be surprised how often that can help?

Do remember, of course, that it is OK to change your mind. Sometimes going through the ABCs helps you to work out the emotion, so don't be afraid to change your mind in the light of new evidence.

Identifying the emotional and behavioural consequences can help you to identify the irrational belief. However, having worked out what the feeling is don't be surprised if sometimes, once you start checking out the inference, you discover that there is another emotion that you experience. If that happens you can choose to work on the new feeling using the ABCs, or stick with the first one and come back to the new one later, whichever you prefer.

More detail about rational and irrational beliefs

Dr Albert Ellis initially pioneered rational emotive behaviour therapy. He noted that there are two kinds of belief: rational beliefs, labelled rBs for short, and irrational beliefs, labelled iBs. Both are evaluations of situations, not descriptions or predictions of them.

How do we define these two types of belief?

First, we will define a rational belief, then an irrational belief.

A rational belief is logical in the sense that the belief is coherent and sensible. It is also realistic: in other words it can be supported by evidence. A rational belief is not absolute or dogmatic, it is relative, conditional and flexible, and it is stated as a *preference*, a *desire* or a *wish*.

A rational belief produces adaptive or helpful emotions: rBs can lead to negative feelings which can range from mild to strong, but which will not be self-defeating for the person. Thus rational beliefs do not lead to the absence of emotion; in fact, it is hard to see how the absence of emotion could be helpful.

Adaptive emotions act as motivators to problem-solving, whereas emotional disturbance usually reduces our ability to problem-solve and often reduces our motivation even to try to problem-solve.

Finally, rational beliefs help us to reach our goals and work towards our interests. Rational beliefs are helpful in producing satisfaction with life, motivation to change when dissatisfied, enhancing problem-solving skills, minimising psychological pain, and helping us to enjoy pleasant social relationships and personal fulfilment.

On the other hand, irrational beliefs are just the opposite.

An irrational belief is logically inconsistent, the conclusion reached is inaccurate and is often an over-generalisation or exaggeration of reality.

An iB is inconsistent with empirical reality; that is, it does not follow from actual events. Irrational beliefs are absolute and dogmatic and expressed as *absolute shoulds* (rather than preferences), *musts* (rather than wishes) and *needs* (rather than desires).

Irrational beliefs are usually habits: that means that they are highly practised and rehearsed, often over a period of many years. They are based on three kinds of demands or *musts* placed on the self, other people or the world in general:

1. I must (for example, be approved of).
2. You must (for example, love me above all else).
3. The world should (for example, give me what I want quickly and easily).

As iBs are illogical and inconsistent with empirical reality (meaning the way the world actually is), it is quite possible to have conflicting irrational beliefs. For example: 'I must be liked by everyone' and 'I must get to be a success no matter what'.

Irrational beliefs lead to damaging emotions and self-defeating actions such as anxiety. Anxiety is debilitating at worst and unhelpful at best.

Finally, irrational beliefs do not help us get to our goal or pursue our interests. When we are stuck in absolute *musts, needs, shoulds, ought to's, got to be's,* and fraught by painful emotions, we are clearly not at our best to say the least! We are not in a position to increase pleasure and minimise discomfort or pain.

Beliefs are either rational (preferring) or irrational (demanding)

Beliefs, then, are philosophies of life based on evaluations of events either past, present or future. There are two types of belief: rational and irrational. The main difference between these two is that the rational beliefs are based on non-dogmatic *preferences*, *desires* and *wants*, whereas irrational beliefs are based on dogmatic *absolute shoulds* or *musts*, *demands* and *needs*.

In looking out for an irrational belief Dr Ellis advises us to look for *musts* and *absolute shoulds*. Especially when you are learning to identify irrational beliefs this a a very helpful tip and can give you good clues to a dogmatic and demanding philosophy.

But it is possible to use the words 'should' and 'must' in a rational way. For instance, if we say 'My carpet is a mess; we should get the vacuum cleaner out', we are probably not making a demand. We are really saying: 'If we want a cleaner carpet we had better vacuum it.'

Likewise, if we say 'You really must go and see Hamlet', we don't really mean that you absolutely have to go; we command it. We mean: 'We liked the play and we think you will, too.'

So don't teach yourself never to say 'should' and never to say 'must' – they are perfectly acceptable English words. Instead look for the meaning behind the words. If you mean them as a sort of commandment they represent a dogmatic demanding philosophy and are therefore showing that you have identified an irrational belief.

At this point let us remind you of insight 3 in Chapter 2.

You have irrational beliefs because you are human and all humans have a biological tendency to think irrationally, although some people have this tendency to a greater degree than others.

This is not, however, the only reason why you have irrational beliefs. You, like all other humans, are very good at learning things – the brain is a great learning device. Our culture frequently reinforces this basic tendency.

For instance, how often do you see pictures or advertisements which suggest that you should be thin, beautiful, graceful, intelligent, admired, etc. When you meet the person who fulfils all these things if you put them in a sideshow next to the elephant man, the incredible bearded lady and the amazing talking fish, you'll make a mint!

In the same view, how many pop songs tell us that absolutely all we have to do to be able to be happy ever after, with never a care in the world, is to meet the right person and sail off into the sunset. Well, if you get there book a ticket for us!

In other words, our culture exaggerates and encourages our own natural tendency to think in a dogmatic, demanding, inflexible, irrational manner.

Demands and their derivatives

Several psychologists have noted that the main component of an irrational belief is its demanding nature; in other words, the tendency to make demands instead of wishes or preferences. They have also noted that there are other parts to irrational beliefs which are usually called 'derivatives'.

Dr Ellis suggests that all emotional trouble has a single cause, that is, demandingness, and that the derivatives follow on from demandingness. Our advice is that when you are identifying an irrational belief look for the demanding philosophy and the derivatives as well.

Demand:	'I must have my boss's approval.'
First derivative:	Awfulising or catastrophising: 'It is absolutely terrible if I have not got her approval.'

Awfulising is an extreme negative evaluation. It is extreme because it probably is bad and disadvantageous if your boss does not approve of you. But when someone is thinking irrationally they take a bad event and convince themselves that it is more than bad, it's absolutely awful. It is 101% bad and it absolutely should not be as it is.

Second derivative:	Low frustration tolerance: 'I can't stand it if she doesn't approve of me, it's too much to bear.'

Low frustration tolerance involves people convincing themselves that it is impossible for them to withstand the discomfort and unpleasantness of an activating event.

Third derivative:	Rating human worth: 'I am a no-good failure if she does not approve of me.' or: 'She is a worthless good-for-nothing if she does not approve of me.'

Rating human worth involves a generalised denigration or condemnation either of one's self or of some other person, and is a major source of irrationality.

An example of ABCs with the full irrational belief

Let's put an example into the ABCs:

A:	**Event:**	The boss tells me she does not like the report I did.
	Inference:	She thinks I am no use.
C:	**Emotional consequence**:	I feel anxious.
	Behavioural consequence:	Blush, stutter.
iB:	'I must have my boss's approval. It's absolutely terrible if she	

thinks I'm no good. If she does think I'm no good that means I'm a failure. I can't stand it if she thinks I'm no good.'

This irrational belief produces the emotional and behavioural consequences and is most unlikely to help in resolving the difficulty. In fact, if the person continues to hold on to, or believe, this irrational belief his or her work is likely to get worse.

When you are working at identifying your own irrational beliefs you will be well advised to look for the demanding philosophy. Ask yourself: 'What am I demanding of myself or of someone else, or of the world in general?'

Once you spot the demand implicit in your thinking write it down and look for any, or all, of the derivatives. When you find that you are awfulising, expressing low frustration tolerance or rating human worth, write them down along with the demand. Please be aware that it is not necessary to find all the derivatives; sometimes the irrational belief has only one or two of the 'optional extras'. It is, however, very likely that you will always find a demanding philosophy.

Some examples of common irrational beliefs

Most irrational beliefs are idiosyncratic, that is, they are particular and individual to each person. However, Drs Walen, DiGuiseppe and Dryden (1992) point out that there are some irrational beliefs that are very common.

Here are a few examples:

1. **iB:**   I must be loved and approved of by every significant person in my life. If I'm not that is absolutely terrible and it means I am unlovable.

Dr Ellis points out that this is an especially common and troublesome irrational belief which leads to fear or anxiety about rejection, or criticism, or disapproval. People who hold on to this irrational belief are unlikely to behave assertively or stand up for their own wishes and opinions.

2. **iB:**   When other people behave unfairly they absolutely should be punished; they are terrible, no-good swines.

This is another common irrational belief which causes a substantial amount of anger that has detrimental consequences. This does not mean that punishment is irrational. Imposing penalties is an important way to influence other people. For example, if someone is guilty of a violent crime the penalty of imprisonment is probably highly appropriate.

The problem with this belief is the idea that a person is thoroughly bad and absolutely must receive punishment. Behaviour, not people, can be rated: indeed, it is wise to rate behaviour. The behaviour may very well be wrong but the person cannot be condemned totally.

3. **iB:** I must have things the way I like them to be and it's awful when they are not that way.

This irrational belief is often at the bottom of resentful anger or depression based on self pity. This belief is really a demand that the world should be so arranged as to give you what you want.

4. **iB:** I should be very anxious about things that are uncertain and could end up in a terrible disaster.

This belief is a demand for complete certainty in our lives, a demand for an absolute guarantee that bad things will not happen. This belief results in anxiety when the guarantee is not forthcoming. It can result in requests for constant reassurance, and in frequent or obsessional checking.

It is also based on a demand that: 'I must be able to ward off or prevent anything bad and if I can't I'm no good.' This belief often causes feelings of guilt and can result in obsessional checking.

5. **iB:** I must be successful and achieving at all times, or at least in one major area, and if I'm not I am worthless.

This is another very common belief and is perhaps especially common in very competitive people or cultures. It is linked to strong fear of, or anxiety about, the possibility of failure, not only because people fear failure but also because they convince themselves that failure makes them – that is, their whole self – worthless.

This example of rating human worth is very anxiety-provoking when people anticipate failure, and results in depression when they actually experience failure.

6. **iB:** There must be a perfect solution to every problem, and I must find it and have complete control over things.

This has two parts: first, the dogmatic demand for a perfect solution, and second, the dogmatic demand for control. It is often linked with a dogmatic demand for certainty and is therefore at the core of anxiety and obsessional checking.

If a person holds this irrational belief she can also experience great difficulty in making decisions, because the decision she makes might not result in the perfect solution, as it absolutely must! If the person has a demanding philosophy directed at others – 'You must find the perfect solution' – she is likely to experience anger.

7. iB: I should be comfortable and without pain or discomfort at all times.

Often this irrational belief refers to psychological and physical pain, discomfort or inconvenience.

If you convince yourself that you have very little ability to stand discomfort and that you should not have to put up with discomfort, this is a form of low frustration tolerance which can lead to addictions such as over-eating, and can make it very difficult for you to engage in any mid- to long-term goals that are likely to result in some discomfort or inconvenience along the way, until the eventual realisation of the good.

Please do not have the impression that these seven examples of some of the some common irrational beliefs represent a complete or exhaustive list. They do not. They will help you to recognise the kind of beliefs that you are looking for.

Chapter 5 will help you to understand how to go about changing irrational beliefs, but in the meantime you might want to use the form at the end to help you practise identifying your own irrational beliefs.

Remember insight 4: it takes hard work and practice; the more you practise the better you will get at it – but how is this for another irrational belief:

iB: 'I must be able to do this immediately, or at least very quickly, and if I can't I am no good?'

Appendix: form 2 for practising ABCs

The problem I want to work on is:

A: Event: . . . .
Inference   1
               2
               3
               4
               etc.

The consequences are:

C: Emotional consequence
      Behavioural consequence
My goal is to feel . . . . and do . . . .

iB: Demand

1. Awfulising/Catastrophising
2. Self or other rating
3. Low frustration tolerance.

Some examples of the use of form 2

Event: My partner is two hours late home from work.
Inference 1:   Maybe the car broke down.
Inference 2:   She is probably cold and frightened in case anything bad
                    happens.
Inference 3:   She might get attacked.
Inference 4:   I might never see her again.

The consequences are:

C: Anxiety
          Dash out to try and find her.

My goal is to feel: Concerned.
 To do: Ring her work to see if they know of any problem.

iB: Demand: I must not lose her; I need her to be with me.
                  If I lost her, it would be the end of the world.
                  I could not bear the loneliness.
                  I am worthless without her.

Event: Check that the gas oven is switched off for the tenth time
                    in ten minutes.
Inference 1:   I may not have switched it off properly.
Inference 2:   Someone would get hurt if it exploded.
Inference 3:   It would be my fault.
Inference 4:   I'd be arrested and locked away.

The consequences are:

C: Anxiety
          Check the oven yet again.

My goal is to feel: Concerned.
To do: Check it once then leave it alone.

iB: Demand: I have to be absolutely sure I've switched it off.
                  Unless I can have absolute certainty, something horrible
                  will happen.
                  I cannot bear the slightest possibility that I made a
                  mistake.

Chapter 5
Disputing irrational beliefs and working at change

When you get to this stage you really begin to appreciate how important insight numbers 3 and 4 are to the process of making changes. This is usually where the hard work of therapy really begins and your therapist will work hard in helping you to put in the necessary effort.

Usually, your therapist will recommend homework assignments which are very important for disputing irrational beliefs and working at change; these homework assignments give you an important opportunity to put into practice the things that you learn in therapy.

Your irrational beliefs represent a philosophy that you have probably lived by for a long time, so they are not easy to change. If you stick at it, with hard work, continuous practice and the help of your therapist, we think that you will have a good chance to get the results that you are after.

This chapter helps you to learn how to go about changing the irrational beliefs.

Recognise the difference between rational and irrational beliefs and practise rational beliefs

People rarely make changes in something unless they have at least some idea of the thing that they are changing to. Given that it takes effort and hard work to change, people only usually make the effort once they have a reasonable idea of what the outcome will be when they have 'changed'.

For example, if someone is thinking of changing his job he is most unlikely to take a job that he knows absolutely nothing about. This same idea applies to changing our philosophy, that is, changing our irrational beliefs.

The first step in changing irrational beliefs is to work out what you will put in their place. Your first question is 'Change the irrational belief into what?'. The answer, of course, is to change the irrational belief into a rational belief.

7. **iB:** I should be comfortable and without pain at all times.

   rB: There is not usually any gain without pain. I would prefer to be comfortable but I do not absolutely have to be. If I am presently uncomfortable that, then, is reality. Demanding that I be comfortable will not change reality but it will worsen my discomfort. I do not like discomfort but I can put up with it. I can also try to increase my comfort while tolerating my discomfort.

This belief acknowledges reality, recognises healthy preferences and disputes a dogmatic demand. It also acknowledges that comfort is a want not a need and can be tolerated.

Recognising rational beliefs and practising them by writing them down and reading them over, preferably out loud, is a first step to changing irrational beliefs.

It is also useful to tape-record your rational belief and play it over to yourself. You will probably need to do this several times a day, every day, until the new rational belief becomes familiar to you.

This is only the first step. It goes hand in hand with the skills of disputing irrational beliefs which are described in the next section of the chapter.

Disputing irrational beliefs

If you want a nice rose garden there are two things that you will have to do: one is to plant roses and the other is to pull up weeds!

Recognising and practising rational beliefs is the equivalent of planting roses. If you do not kill the weeds the roses will have a difficult time and may even die. Disputing the irrational beliefs is the equivalent of killing the weeds. Both recognising and practising rational beliefs and disputing irrational beliefs are necessary for making changes.

The process of disputing involves debating with or challenging your irrational belief system. You take a good look at each irrational belief and explore the extent to which they make sense and are helpful.

Stop and *think*, and teach yourself a new philosophy. This is part of removing irrational beliefs and teaching yourself rational beliefs.

Drs Walen, DiGuiseppe and Dryden (1992) point out that it is possible to engage in this process of disputing irrational beliefs at different levels of abstraction. An irrational belief may be specific or it may be increasingly abstract.

An example of a specific irrational belief would be: 'My partner absolutely should have shown me respect the other evening when I asked him to get our guests a drink.' If you go about disputing a specific belief such as this you will enable yourself to cope better, if and when he fails to show you respect under similar circumstances.

An example of an abstract belief might be: 'People must show me respect.' If you dispute this abstract belief you will teach yourself to cope better when your partner or anyone else fails to show you respect.

The more specific the irrational belief that you dispute the more specific you will be in the results you get. Put another way, the more narrow the irrational belief you dispute the more limited your results.

If you try to dispute less specific, more general or abstract irrational beliefs you will get results that help you in more than one situation. Therefore it is good advice to try to direct your efforts towards more abstract or general irrational beliefs.

Nevertheless, do not neglect specific beliefs entirely, particularly in the early stages of therapy. You may find that it is best to work on both specific and general irrational beliefs, but to concentrate a little more of your efforts on the latter.

When you are disputing, write down the irrational belief that you want to dispute at the top of a sheet of paper. The next step is to ask questions of the belief.

There are, broadly speaking, three kinds of questions that you will want to ask yourself about the irrational belief:

1. Questions about its logic
2. Questions about its realism
3. Questions about its helpfulness.

Question whether the irrational belief is logical

The first criterion of rational thinking is that it is logical which, usually, irrational beliefs are not. Questions about logic focus on whether the irrational belief logically follows from the reasoning that you use to defend it.

Dr Albert Ellis recognised some time ago that if you take an irrational belief such as 'I must have my boss's approval', and you ask why the person must have his boss's approval, he will probably provide the following answers:

'Because if I don't I may not get promoted' *or*
'Because work will be unpleasant if he dislikes me' *or*
'Because if he doesn't like me he will give me a bad reference.'

Dr Ellis would probably point out that all these would be reasons why it would be preferable or desirable to have the boss's approval. In other words, this shows that the following rational belief, 'I would like to have the boss's approval because it will probably be advantageous', is logical.

But back to the irrational belief. Why must you have it? It is relatively easy to realise that just because something is preferable or desirable that it does not mean that you must have it.

If you desire that you find £10 000 in your waste paper bin, left there

by the good fairies, it does not logically follow that you must find
£10 000.

Desirability and reality have no logical relationship to each other. If
there were a logical relationship between them we would always get
something merely by wanting it!

Another form of logical dispute is to point out ways in which the irrational belief is not consistent. For example, many people have one stan-
dard for themselves ('I must be perfect') and another for everyone else
('You did your best; that's all anyone can expect').

Or, 'You must not let me down, but if I let you down it was because of
unfortunate circumstances'.

It is important when disputing to keep stressing to yourself logical
inconsistencies in your irrational beliefs.

When you see the irrational belief written down in front of you some
of the disputing questions that you ask yourself about it might include
the following:

> Is that good logic?
> How do I know?
> Why does that follow?
> Might I be over-generalising?
> If a friend had that belief would I accept it?

Question whether the irrational belief is realistic

Irrational beliefs can also be challenged on empirical or realistic
grounds. Ask yourself: Is the belief consistent with actual reality?

When scientists do experiments they do not tell us what they wanted
or expected to find out, but what in reality they did find out.

One criterion of irrational beliefs is that they are often not consistent
with reality. For instance, take the belief, 'I should be 6 feet tall'. As you
are actually 5 feet 7 inches, this belief is not consistent with reality.

You may have a preference, 'I would like to be 6 feet tall'. That rational belief is consistent with reality because the reality is not your
height but your preference. Therefore a rational belief usually is consistent with reality whereas an irrational belief is not.

In disputing an irrational belief it is important to accept reality as it is,
not to demand the reality that you want. This, of course, does not mean
that we advise you to resign yourself to the reality; once you have
accepted reality you can make every effort to change your circumstances.

If the circumstances cannot be changed – for instance, your height –
then accept them as they are and get on with the rest of your life without
demanding that reality should not be reality! No matter how strongly
you make this demand it will not have any impact one way or the other
on the reality.

This kind of dispute can be used with irrational beliefs such as: 'My partner absolutely should do more around the house.'

Ask yourself, in reality does she or he do more around the house at this time? If the answer is 'No', then that is reality; accept it and try to get him or her to change. If he or she will not do more around the house no matter what you do, you can put up with that little bit of reality or you can leave.

Your first step had better be to accept reality!

When you are using this kind of dispute, write down the irrational belief in front of you, think like a scientist and ask yourself the following questions:

> Where is this law written down?
> What do the data show?
> Where's the evidence?
> Why must he or she do that?
> Is it true?
> Is there a universal law that says that it's true?

Question whether or not the irrational belief is helpful to you

The third criterion of rational beliefs, as well as being logical and realistic, is that they should help you to achieve your goals, behave in a coping way and experience healthy negative emotions in response to bad events.

When you agree to dispute an irrational belief on the grounds of whether it is helpful, ask yourself: 'How does this idea help me?' How does the irrational belief help you to solve problems?

Does the idea bring about any healthy or helpful feelings, and when you think that way how do you act?

For example, take the irrational belief: 'I must not make any mistakes at work.'

If you think that way how will you feel? Probably anxious in case you make mistakes, which also means that you'll be more likely to make mistakes because of loss of concentration. After you make a mistake you may feel ashamed or embarrassed and try to hide the mistake. Or if someone else points out a mistake that you have made you may feel angry and shout at him or her.

As before, if you are using this type of dispute write down the irrational belief that you want to give up and then ask yourself questions about it, for example:

> As long as I believe that how will I feel?
> Where will that demand get me?
> How does that idea motivate me?

Summary: disputing questions

When disputing an irrational belief it is usually best to use all these three approaches. Recall the insights in Chapter 2, however. You will probably have to work long and hard with frequent practice and repetitions; do not expect to give up the beliefs easily and without a struggle, because they are ingrained habits.

Remember, too, that disputing irrational beliefs is not enough to change them. Unless you have new ideas to replace the old irrational beliefs you are not likely to change them. If you try using disputing with rational beliefs you will find that rational beliefs usually are logical, realistic and helpful.

It may be useful to try comparing the irrational belief with the rational belief and think about which belief is better and why.

Disputing the core elements

The core elements of irrational beliefs were described in Chapter 4 and are the demands and the derivatives. Below is a description of the core elements.

Demandingness

This is the belief in universal absolutes or musts.

Awfulising

This is the belief that the world is full of horrible, awful, catastrophic things.

Low frustration tolerance

This the belief that one cannot bear what one does not like.

Human worth ratings

This is the belief that people can be rated.

Below are some examples of irrational beliefs which have got all four core elements:

> Other people should love me.
> It's awful when they don't.
> I can't bear not being loved.
> I'm worthless if I'm not loved.

or

> He should not act that way; he has no right.
> It's awful that he acts that way.
> I can't stand it when people don't do what I want.
> He is a completely bad person for acting that way.

or

> It should not have happened because it's not fair and it should be.
> It's awful when I get things I don't deserve.
> I can't stand unfairness.
> The world is just no good.

Let's look at each of the core elements of irrational beliefs in turn.

Disputing the demands

Disputing the demands is very important to the process of personal growth and making changes. It will form a cornerstone of your therapy.

When you are looking for irrational beliefs that you are going to change look for the following words in your thoughts: must, absolutely should, ought to, have to and need. Musts are often made about things that happened in the past when people have painful negative emotions such as depression, anger, hurt and guilt, or about present and future events if you are feeling anxious.

Most irrational beliefs reveal a philosophy of demand rather than one of preference; as Dr Ellis puts it: 'My will be done!'

Often when Dr Ellis is helping people to change irrational beliefs he helps them to recognise that just because they want something there is no logical reason why they have to have it. You may very much want £1000 to fall out of the sky and land in your lap, but does your wanting it mean that therefore it will definitely happen?

When you have disputed your philosophy of demandingness the key is to understand the difference between wants or preferences, on the one hand, and needs or demands, on the other.

Wants and preferences involve objects, events or relationships that we would like to have, that would enrich our lives and encourage increased happiness.

Alternatively, wants and preferences can also concern things that we would like not to have or not to happen, because if they do they will reduce our comfort or satisfaction and be detrimental in some way.

On the other hand, needs or musts are things that if we do not have we will die. Human beings have very many things that constitute genuine wants or preferences, but there are very few things that we genuinely need or must or must not have.

The only genuine needs or musts are air, water, food and, in certain climates, shelter and clothes. Anything else that you can think of is a want or a preference.

Wants and preferences are healthy, acceptable and need not be disputed. They constitute a person's values: values can, of course, be changed, but it is quite possible to have any want or preference and stay mentally healthy, even if you do not have the thing you desire. It is when people change their healthy preferences into a 'got to be', into a philosophy of demandingness, that they get into trouble with their mental health.

The first step in changing a demand is to be alert to this idea: is the thing you are currently demanding really a necessity or is it actually a preference? We think that if you practise careful thinking you will see that it is a preference, albeit perhaps a strong preference.

Many people believe that there are laws which must be followed whether they are religious or legal ones. From the REBT point of view, these laws are not absolutely natural universal laws of nature which must be followed; they are laws devised by people.

Please do not think that we are saying that they are unimportant; we are not.

Take the law that you must not kill people. Obviously it is very important to obey this law but, sadly, as we see in the news practically every day people break it.

The fact that human beings are capable of killing does not mean that this law is of no use or that it can be cheerfully ignored. It is a wise person who obeys this law and a just society that polices it, but there is no law of nature that makes killing impossible.

It is therefore rational and healthy to acknowledge that you, and indeed most people, have a very strong preference never to kill anyone and for others never to kill too, but sadly there is no universal law to say that it absolutely must not happen.

When someone does take a life, that is, they transgress this very important legal code, we very much hope that they will be subjected to a fair judicial process and be severely penalised for their crime.

The same kind of argument applies to ethical and religious laws: there is nothing to say that they absolutely must be observed, but a wise and healthy person will have a strong preference to behave ethically and a person who practises a religious faith will have a strong preference to follow the teachings of his religion.

Therefore, we distinguish between the advisability of a particular behaviour and the person's ability to choose; it is possible for a person to choose not to follow legal, ethical or religious codes.

I must, you must, it must

One kind of 'must' statement is made about one's self and constitutes a demand for perfection along with failure to acknowledge human fallibility.

If you want to change this kind of demanding philosophy you should recognise that human beings are not perfect. Although it is possible to do our best and to improve upon our best, it is not possible for human beings to be perfect. We are, by our very nature, imperfect.

Take the irrational belief, 'I must be perfect', and apply it to the questions discussed previously in this chapter.

Is the belief logical? It is not. It is logical to say that I have a desire to do my best but I do not have to be perfect. Although my desire to do my best follows from my own preference, it does not logically follow that just because I want to do my best I must do so.

If the demand did logically follow from the preference I would have to do my best whether I wanted to or not; it would be impossible not to do my best. There is a natural law stating that on earth objects must fall to the ground, but there is no equivalent law saying that I must do my best.

Is the belief realistic? No! If it were, I would always do my best no matter what the circumstances. In reality I do not always do my best. The belief 'I prefer to do my best' is realistic in that I do have a preference.

Finally, how does the demand help me? It does not help at all; demanding that I always do my best under all conditions results in me feeling anxious, not concentrating properly and therefore making more mistakes.

If the rational belief 'I strongly prefer to do my best but I do not absolutely have to' is subjected to the same questions, you will see that it is logical, realistic and helpful.

Rational belief: I prefer to do my best but neither I nor anyone else is perfect. Human beings make mistakes. There is no law to say I must be perfect. If I tell myself I must be perfect I will suffer.

A second type of demanding philosophy can be about other people, and this usually demands perfection from others. If you want to change this kind of demanding philosophy, recognise that other people have free will: they can make choices and we cannot have complete control over the choices that they make.

If we try to exert complete control over other people's choices, negative results usually follow in that the other person usually resists us in some way and we experience a painful negative emotion such as anger; we may even lose our temper.

When someone behaves in a way that we don't like it is very common to hear people say: 'How could they do that?' Surprisingly, the answer is: 'They can do it easily because they can do anything they choose.'

This, of course, does not mean that it is acceptable or wise for them to behave that way.

Consider: 'How can terrorists plant bombs?' Answer: 'They can do it easily but this does not mean that they have a right to do it, or that it is a wise course of action for them to take.'

Another typical question is: 'Why do they do this?' There are many possible answers to this question. Perhaps they believe that it will bring them some kind of benefit; perhaps they are disturbed; people may behave badly because they are ignorant of some things or they are misinformed.

There are many ways in which we could explain their behaviour, but whichever explanation we choose will not actually alter the behaviour.

Imagine, for example, that you lend someone £100.00 and he refuses to repay it; you feel angry and have the irrational belief: 'He absolutely should not take me for granted.'

Is the belief logical? No! It is logical to believe that 'It is preferable he does not take me for granted', but just because it is preferable does not mean he must not do so. To believe that 'because it is preferable that he does not take me for granted he must not do so' is magical thinking.

There is no logical relationship at all between preferences and demands. Simply demanding that something is so will not make it so. The demand per se will have no impact on reality.

Is it realistic? Again, no! If the person did take you for granted, that is reality and cannot be changed either by thinking or acting. If something – in this case being taken for granted – happened, it should have simply been because it did happen. All the factors were in place to make it happen. Reality should be as it is.

How does thinking 'he must not take me for granted' help? It does not. The dogmatic belief will not alter the facts but will result in an unhealthy negative emotion which will not only feel highly unpleasant but will make it harder to devise ways to reduce the likelihood of being taken for granted in the future.

Rational belief: 'I strongly prefer that he does not take me for granted, but there is nothing to say that he must do as I wish.'

In this case, if you think rationally you will feel annoyed but not angry that he has not returned the loan. Feeling annoyed will foster your assertion skills, and if he refuses to return your money it will motivate you not to lend him any more in the future!

Furthermore, it will remind you that, just like you, he is not perfect; he can behave, and on this occasion has behaved, imperfectly.

The third form of demanding philosophy is that people demand that they control inanimate objects, social institutions and general circumstances.

How often do you hear people say: 'It's not fair; it shouldn't happen to me!' The main way of dealing with this kind of demand is to recognise that the world does not revolve around you or exist for your own satisfaction.

Unfortunately, the world often, but not always, is unfair. That is reality.

Another form of demand in this category is: 'It's not fair; I don't deserve this, so I shouldn't have to put up with it!' We do not always get what we 'deserve'; that is the way of the world. That is reality.

In a sense we do not deserve anything; what happens happens regardless of whether we deserve it. As before, in this sense it is not always fair, but it does not have to be fair. Fairness is, however, desirable.

Consider the situation that your car has broken down and you are stuck on the side of the motorway, late for an appointment and feeling furious. You sit in your car, waiting for the repair service, thinking the following irrational belief:

Irrational belief: 'It's not fair that my car breaks down now of
                          all times. This should not be happening to me.'

Is it logical to say that this should not be happening?

No, there is no law to say that your car must never break down, that it must work perfectly; and there is no law to say that life has got to be fair. Just because you want it to be fair it does not follow that it has to be.

There is no law to say it must not happen to you now or at any other time. You may very well dislike this strongly, but there is no law to say that you absolutely have to have only things that you like to happen.

Is the belief realistic? No, it is realistic to believe that the car has broken down. Indeed, as it has broken down it is actually realistic to say that it should have broken down. Why? As it has broken down, there is something wrong with it; it is faulty. If it is faulty it probably should break down because the circumstances are all in place to result in a break down.

Does telling yourself it should not happen get it fixed any quicker? No! Does telling yourself that it should not happen help you to maintain a stable blood pressure? Probably not! Does it, in fact, help you in any way? Probably not.

It merely results in you sitting in a broken-down car waiting for a repair service, still getting later and later for your appointment, and on top of all that you feel more and more angry!

Rational belief: 'I wish my car had not broken down at such
                        an inconvenient time, but it has and there is
                        nothing to say that it must not have done. It
                        may well be unfair, but whoever said the
                        world has to be fair. I would prefer for this
                        not to be happening to me but it is and there

> is nothing to say that it should not be. In fact,
> if the car is faulty it probably should break
> down sooner or later.'

If you think rationally you are still sitting in a broken-down car, but at least you no longer feel furious, although perhaps you do feel irritated. It may also help to motivate you to get the car serviced more often!

Disputing the derivatives

Awfulising

Awfulising is a common factor in unhealthy emotion and happens when people exaggerate the badness of things or blow things out of proportion. Often people use words such as 'awful', 'terrible' and 'horrible' in a loose, undefined way. They use these words when they really mean that something is disadvantageous, undesirable or very bad, but at times of irrationality people hold the philosophy that it is 'more than bad', it is 'the end of the world' and believe that 'it should not be this bad'.

In essence, their philosophy is that 'awful' means absolutely, totally bad, the worst thing that could ever happen. This implies that it is 101% bad which is, of course, impossible. They also tend to add that it should not be so bad.

People rarely awfulise about positive or beneficial things; awfulising only comes about when our goals or interests are blocked in negative situations. In such cases 'it' may indeed be bad, but it cannot be 'too bad' or 'more than bad'.

If something is undesirable, disadvantageous or bad for you, then that is what it is; convincing yourself that it is more than bad will only make it worse. Insisting that it should not be so bad is also nonsense. People often adopt two strategies to deal with awfulising, neither of which will work.

On the one hand, they try very hard not to think about the 'awful' thing. Each time it comes into their mind they remind themselves that it is awful and that therefore they must not think about it. This strategy is typical of anxiety and its effect is that the person thinks about the 'awful' thing more and more, and each time they think about it, it gets even more 'awful' in their mind.

On the other hand, they might try telling themselves that it isn't really so bad; in fact, it's pretty trivial, nothing to get het up about. This is the so-called power of positive thinking. It does not usually work because the issue is not trivial to them: it is important and it is bad. Most people cannot fool themselves for very long.

So what is the alternative?

The alternative is to think about the bad event rationally and put it in its non-exaggerated, rightful context, that is, to recognise that although it may be bad or undesirable, it is not more than bad, it is not the end of the world and it is not 'awful'.

One way of doing this is by making a comparison of this event with other bad events using a scale of badness.

For example, suppose Anne's boss criticises her and clearly disapproves of something she has done. She tells herself the following irrational belief:

iB: 'It is terrible that my boss disapproves of me. It's not just bad it's the end of the world; I've had it now.'

Consequently she feels very anxious. Now think about the badness scale of 0–100% (Figure 5.1).

Figure 5.1

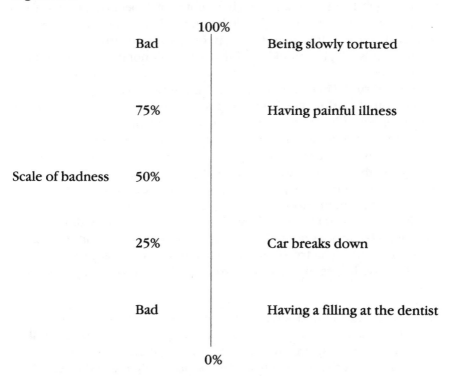

Several 'bad events' are placed on the scale of badness at where we judge to be their rightful place. So, having a filling at the dentist is not fun, it is a bad event; but it is not actually a very bad event – it doesn't usually hurt, it is over quickly and produces only mild discomfort. So we judge it to be only 10% bad. But it is still on the scale of badness.

Let us suppose that being tortured slowly is 100% bad; it is very bad but, by definition, it cannot be more than 100% bad because 100% is the maximum in badness. On this scale where does the war in Bosnia or Rwanda belong? Where does the Zeebrugge ferry disaster belong?

And, finally, where does Anne's being disapproved of by the boss belong?

Hopefully, this will help you put being disapproved of by the boss in its rightful place: it is a bad, undesirable event, but it is hardly the end of the world, and it is not awful, horrible or terrible.

Another way of dealing with awfulising is to use the three disputing arguments. Let's take as an example the following irrational belief:

iB: 'It's terrible that my boss disapproves of me. It's not just
        bad, it's the end of the world. I've had it now.'

Is this logical? Is it really 'the end of the world'? That phrase means it is more than 100% bad and that is magical thinking. It is not possible for something to be more than 100% bad. If it is bad, believing that it is too bad is also illogical, in that it should be only as bad as it is simply because it is. That is reality. It is logical to deny, or to demand, that reality should not be as it is. Magical thinking of that kind will not mean it will be bad forever.

Is it realistic? When you think 'I've had it now' what does that actually mean? You are using words very vaguely. In reality, if your boss disapproves of you it is bad and may be disadvantageous: for example, you may lose promotion or have a tense working environment.

But realistically, although that is bad, how bad is it in the scheme of things? On the scale of badness where does it belong? Is it absolutely the worst thing that could happen? It could, in fact, be a lot worse; it is not the worst that could happen.

How is this belief helpful? How does it help you cope with the disapproval? It clearly does not help you cope, it has quite the opposite effect. How does it help you try to regain some measure of his approval? It does not, because it gets in the way of your ability to solve problems effectively:

rB: 'It is bad and undesirable that my boss disapproves of what I did,
        but it is not awful. Unpleasant consequences may indeed follow
        from his disapproval, but that is not the end of the world and
        there is nothing to say that I will be adversely affected forever.'

Of course, this awfulising usually takes place in conjunction with a demand. For example, in this case the demand could be one of the following:

iB: I must have his approval, or
iB: He should not criticise me, or
iB: It should not be so unfair, or

iB: It should not be as bad as this.

As well as disputing the awfulising it would be wise to dispute the demand as well, and replace it with a rational belief which asserts your healthy preference but kicks the demand out, for example:

> 'I would like to have his approval but I do not have to have it', or
> 'I would prefer he did not criticise me but there is no law to say that he must not do so', or
> 'I wish it were fairer, but it does not absolutely have to be', or
> 'It is bad and there is nothing to say that it must not be so bad. I wish it weren't so bad.'

Often, when people get into the habit of awfulising, especially when they get themselves anxious, they demand guarantees. For example, here is a very common irrational belief:

iB: 'It would be absolutely awful if I made a mistake such as leaving the door unlocked when I go out. I need a guarantee that I will not make a mistake and that the door is locked.'

This kind of philosophy leads to obsessive checking in an effort to gain a reassuring 'guarantee'. Unfortunately, each time you check you can only be sure that the door is currently locked: you cannot be sure that you have absolutely, unquestionably, not unlocked it when you checked.

The problem here is the awfulising associated with the demand for a guarantee. Life rarely gives any guarantee and if you recognise this characteristic of yourself, practise disputing both the demand and the awfulising.

Low frustration tolerance

From time to time life is not easy. By circumstances or by our own mistakes and poor decisions, people are often faced with difficulties and frustrations. These difficulties and frustrations get in the way of one's goals and interests, and produce feelings of discomfort.

As frustrations are more or less inevitable, it is wise to learn to deal with them as well as possible by developing a strong ability to tolerate life's frustrations. Many people who are in emotional troubles contribute to their difficulties by having little ability to tolerate frustration: in other words, they have 'low frustration tolerance'.

One indicator of low frustration tolerance is a difficulty in making decisions when your short-term and long-term interests conflict. If you are someone who neglects long-term interests and concentrates on short-term goals, then you probably have taught yourself a philosophy of low frustration tolerance.

This philosophy is typical of people with addiction difficulties, such as over-eating; of people who constantly put things off; of people who easily give up on things when they know that it would be wise to stick at it; and of people who go out of their way to avoid life's hassles even though this strategy makes things worse in the long run.

There are four major irrational beliefs that are part of a low frustration tolerance philosophy. Your therapist will help you look carefully for these and, if you have any, work at changing them.

The first is the irrational belief 'I must not be frustrated'. Along with this irrational demand there is usually the belief that the person absolutely cannot stand frustration and that it is too much to bear.

If you have this philosophy it is important to dispute it; if you don't dispute it you will have a strategy of running for cover and trying to hide from problems whenever they arise. This is unlikely to solve the problem and likely to make it worse.

Ask yourself the following:

> Is it logical that you must not be frustrated?
> Where is the universal law that says that?
> How does this demand help you to get rid of the frustration?
> Is it realistic to say it is too much to bear?

rB: I dislike being frustrated and would prefer not to be, but there is no law to say that I must not be frustrated: if I am, I am. No amount of demanding that it should not happen will make it go away, but I will make it harder for myself to bear. It is hard to bear frustration sometimes, but it is untrue to say that it is too much to bear. If it were too much to bear it would have killed me! Although it may be, in reality, hard to bear, I can make it harder by convincing myself that it is too hard to stand. I can stand it even though I don't like it.

It is important to challenge this 'I can't stand it' philosophy. This philosophy means two things:

1. If in reality you can't stand it, it will, logically, kill you. If it were true to say 'I can't stand frustration' then frustration would be fatal. It is not fatal! It is true to say 'I can't stand being held under water for 20 minutes without breathing apparatus', but it is not true to say 'I can't stand frustration'.
2. It means that unless the frustration goes away immediately you can never experience any degree of happiness again as long as you live.

Although it may be true that frustrations reduce one's happiness they do not blow it out of the water totally, now and forever.

The second irrational belief is 'I must be comfortable now and it would be unbearable if I were not'. If you hold on to this belief you will be very unlikely to do anything that reduces your immediate level of discomfort. Anything that forces you into action will be perceived as an enormous imposition and you will be prone to the unhealthy emotions of anger and depression.

The third irrational belief is 'negative feelings are unbearable and I absolutely should not have to experience them'. This will result in you leading a very narrow, constricted life and cause you to see the threat of negative feelings in many situations.

Also, as negative feelings are inevitable from time to time, this belief will worsen your negative feelings when you do experience them. This belief is very typical of people who experience panic attacks. Panic attacks are caused by self-created anxiety; the person who believes this irrational belief then makes it even worse by thinking: 'This anxiety is unbearable; I can't stand it; it must go immediately. I should not feel anxious.'

The fourth irrational belief is: 'I must experience good feelings; it would be terrible if I don't. Life would be unbearable if I were not constantly happy.'

This belief is most closely linked to addiction to things that bring short-lived feelings of well-being, such as food or alcohol. As they only last briefly, the person quickly learns that he needs a new fix. This becomes dangerous and self-defeating.

If you recognise any or all of these low frustration tolerance beliefs it is wise to work hard and practise disputing them and building up high frustration tolerance with rational beliefs. If you want to know more about this kind of philosophy of life, there is a book about it, called *Beating the Comfort Trap*, by Dr Windy Dryden and Jack Gordon (1993), published by Sheldon Press.

Rating human worth

Dr Albert Ellis, who founded rational emotive behaviour therapy, recognised some time ago that a person's estimation of his or her worth is very important, and that if the person has a poor self-image he or she will suffer from the kind of problems described in Chapter 1.

When someone does not value himself very highly, several other problems will follow. He will concentrate on his own rottenness and pay little attention to problem-solving. He may decide that someone so worthless cannot get anything right and is bound to fail all the time; then he may as well stop trying.

He may try desperately to make others like him, believing that they are bound to see through him one day. He may be very unassertive and always try to let other people have their own way, even if that causes him great problems. He may feel very guilty. He may be rather hostile and aggressive.

Dr Ellis points out that, given the importance of this topic, it has become central to modern psychotherapy; this has led to the following question being asked about the topic: as the person's self-acceptance seems to depend on (1) succeeding or achieving in society or (2) having good relations with others, how can we help a person to improve his self-esteem? Dr Ellis gave this question considerable thought over many years and is generally recognised as an expert in the field.

He asked himself a different question: if a person's perception of his own worth is so important, why does a person foolishly put himself down and how can we help him judge himself so that, no matter how well or how badly he behaves, or how popular or unpopular he is, he accepts or respects himself?

This was a revolutionary way of looking at this problem because Dr Ellis distinguished between self-acceptance and self-esteem, which are not the same.

Self-esteem means that the person values himself because he has done well in some way. This, in itself, may be non-problematic, but taken to its logical extreme it suggests that we will dis-esteem ourselves if we behave badly in some way. Given that human beings are probably incapable of perfection, this suggests that the concept of self-esteem can only exist together with a willingness to put ourselves down. So, although self-esteem may seem like a good thing, it can only be relied upon if you can rely on yourself never to do anything bad, foolish or inappropriate.

By contrast, self-acceptance is healthy. Self-acceptance means that you fully and unconditionally accept yourself whether you act intelligently or stupidly, and whether or not other people approve of you, respect you or love you. Although only well behaving, constantly loved, perfect people genuinely merit self-esteem, all we ordinary mortals are capable of real self-acceptance.

It is irrational to judge or rate one's whole self, although that is precisely what people do when they aim to improve their self-esteem. It is also what they do when they put themselves down.

Why is it irrational to rate your 'self'?

Look around for a few seconds at the room you are sitting in. Now, you can have one word, and only one, to evaluate your surroundings. But your evaluation has to be accurate and complete! Almost certainly you can pick one work to describe the room, but is that one word an accurate and complete description? For example, you could say your room is 'cold', but that does not sum up everything there is to say about the room; it only judges one aspect of the room. To describe the room properly you would need to use a great many words.

The point is that you cannot describe the room in one word because it is too complicated. The room is too detailed to be given a single, simple judgement. Now, you can give yourself a single, simple judgement: you are clever. You say this because you have university degrees. But there is a problem: you are not very good at DIY, painting, fixing things, etc. In fact, you generally do it rather badly; therefore, you must be stupid. So which are you: clever because of your degrees or stupid because you are poor at DIY?

The answer is that, just like the room, you are much too complicated to be give a single judgement of 'self'. My 'self' is made up of thousands of parts, both physical parts such as bones, organs and the like, and psychological parts such as characteristics, preferences and actions.

Both authors of this book have a slight stutter. JT has had his since he was a child and for a long time doggedly convinced himself of this irrational belief:

iB: 'Because I stutter I am no good and no one will ever like me. I must get people to like me; I must not stutter.'

He worked very hard for several years to convince himself that this nonsense was true, and became more and more miserable about his stutter and more afraid of talking, especially on telephones, and the stutter got worse.

When he began to think more rationally his stutter got much better and these days, although he does stutter occasionally, he does so much less and doesn't worry about it.

So what is his healthy rational belief?

rB: 'Having a slight stutter is certainly undesirable and a nuisance, but it does not make me bad. I am a person with good bits and bad bits; one bad or irritating bit does not make me bad. If other people disapprove of me for my stutter, that's their problem. I would like to be approved of, but I certainly do not have to be. I dislike stuttering but if I do I do . . . tough. The planet will not cease to spin on its axis and send me flying off into the cold, dark depths of space.'

The rational belief above describes the development towards self-acceptance rather than self-esteem. It is relatively easy to esteem ourselves for our good points, but it takes practice to develop a healthy self-acceptance. The practice is worth it.

Our advice is: there are no rational grounds for rating or judging your whole self or for judging another person. Work hard to develop the habit of never judging your self no matter what you do, no matter who likes you.

Do not rate people but do judge behaviour

Please do not think all judgement is wrong. Although it is irrational to judge the self it is very wise to judge behaviours and thoughts, both your own and other people's.

For example, although we cannot sensibly judge our whole selves for having university degrees, we can judge our achievements positively and take pride in them. It does not, however, make us better or worse people.

If you go to a party and behave rudely, perhaps getting too drunk and being sick, you can judge the behaviour as bad, apologise and try to make amends, but that does not make the whole of you, now and forever, bad. The act is bad; the person is a person neither good nor bad.

If you think some form of prejudiced thought, the thought is biased and unfair – but you have millions of thoughts over the course of a life-time, some of which are biased, some of which are not. You can recognise your prejudice as bad and try to do something about it.

Similarly, if someone hits you, judge that behaviour: it is bad, undesir-able behaviour but it does not make your attacker thoroughly evil. Given that the behaviour is bad, act appropriately and report the matter to the police!

Usually, rating of human worth goes hand in hand with demands. For example, take a typical angry motorist. Someone is driving behind you, much too close and blowing his horn. Then he swerves past you, blow-ing his horn again and waving his fist. You feel angry at him and your irrational belief is:

iB: 'He should not do this to me; he is a complete sod.'

Try applying the three disputing questions to this belief. The rational belief would be:

rB: 'There is no law to say that he should not behave badly; he is behaving badly and it would be much better if he drove sensibly. His behaviour is bad but he is not a bad person: he is a person who is behaving foolishly and driving badly.'

With this rational belief your anger would change into healthy annoy-ance.

The irrational habit of rating human worth is very common among people, perhaps because so much of our popular culture encourages us to do so. For example, it's often implied that all men must be competitive, macho go-getters, and all women should have a perfect figure, smiles that stop traffic, and love furry animals and little children. And woe betide them if they don't!

Regardless of how irrational cultural expectations can be, you are well advised to get into the habit of never rating yourself or other people, because there is no rational basis upon which to reach a fair judgement.

It is, however, wise to judge thoughts and actions: take pride in your success and disappointment in your failings. Try, non-dogmatically, to modify your weaknesses or faults as best you can. Recognise that your strengths and weaknesses do not make you anything. You are a person with strengths and weaknesses.

There is a book available, written by Dr Paul Hauck (1991), called *Hold Your Head up High*, and published by Sheldon Press.

Disputing irrational beliefs through actions and experience

It is very rarely enough to dispute your irrational beliefs by talking yourself out of them. This is an important part of the disputing process but it is rarely sufficient. The chances are that for a long time you have been thinking and acting in ways that strengthen your actual beliefs.

Now that you are making changes, you will need to work just as hard at thinking and acting according to your rational beliefs. It is very likely that your therapist will suggest behavioural homework assignments for you to do outside the therapy session, because acting against your irrational beliefs is a powerful way to make changes.

Challenging but not overwhelming

We believe that when you act on your own rational beliefs the principle of 'challenging but not overwhelming' is important. When taking action and changing your behaviour there are three ways to proceed:

1. Jump in at the deep end. This involves repeatedly and frequently doing the actions that you usually avoid; indeed it involves directly confronting the situation you most fear. This is a very good and quick way to make changes, and it is very helpful if you can do it. But many people feel they cannot 'jump in at the deep end'.
2. Take very slow and tiny steps. This involves breaking the action down in to very small, manageable parts and then doing a part of the behav-

iour you feel that you can do comfortably. This method will work, but only very slowly. It has the important disadvantage that it will possibly reinforce your low frustration tolerance which is probably already a big part of your problem.

3. Challenge but don't overwhelm yourself. This involves taking action somewhere between the two extremes described above. Although you do not jump in at the deep end, you do undertake action that will not be easy but will be challenging. This has the advantage of helping you to make behavioural changes while also working against your low frustration tolerance.

In our experience most people in therapy opt for the challenging but not overwhelming principle. Your therapist will help you to work out what this means for you in practice.

Whichever of the three you choose you will probably not make any powerful and long-lasting changes unless you engage in action and then practise disputing your irrational beliefs while acting in accordance with your rational beliefs.

An example of this principle involved me (JT) overcoming my anxiety about stuttering. The thing that helped most was challenging my irrational beliefs while lecturing to fairly small groups of students at college. This involved a challenge but did not overwhelm me. Later, when this action was progressing, I pushed myself into a greater challenge which involved lecturing to groups of 40 or 50 students. While I stood in front of the class I practised working against my irrational beliefs.

I did not do this public speaking once or twice, but many times, and this is another important aspect of therapy; change involves repeated action; one-off attempts are rarely sufficient. While acting, it is important to rehearse your rational beliefs.

Disputing irrational beliefs through visual imagery

Sometimes an easier step before actions is to practise the action in the mind's eye. This type of 'visual imagery' can be very useful and it is quite probable that your therapist will advise you to use it during therapy and/or as a homework exercise.

Dr Ellis, and a colleague of his, Dr Maultsby, developed the use of visual imagery in therapy. There are, broadly speaking, two kinds of imagery: negative and positive.

Negative rational–emotive imagery

In this type of imagery you close your eyes and try to imagine yourself in any problem situation (A), and then try to experience the unhealthy emotions (C) that you usually feel in that situation. Once you feel the emotion try to change it to a healthy negative emotion. It may seem strange at first, but with practice you can do it.

When you have changed the feeling your therapist will ask you how you did it. If you were successful you will find that you changed your irrational belief to a rational one.

If you changed the problem, that is, changed the A, go back and try to do it again without changing A. This is a good way to practise your rational beliefs and to practise changing your irrational beliefs.

Positive rational–emotive imagery

In this kind of imagery you imagine yourself in a typical problem situation (A), but then you imagine yourself thinking rationally (B) about it. This will help you to cope with the situation and feel a healthy negative emotion about the situation. You do not have to imagine yourself coping perfectly; rarely, if ever, do people cope perfectly with anything!

It is quite probable that your therapist will discuss these and other imagery techniques with you in therapy.

The importance of homework

Homework exercises, that is, exercises for you to do between therapy sessions, are a very important part of therapy. Your chances of making changes without doing homework exercises are very much less than they are if you do them.

Homework exercises will be used to help you to dispute your irrational beliefs. They may involve keeping records, writing notes, disputing beliefs on paper, reading books or carrying out actions. These are just some examples.

Your therapist will negotiate the homework with you so that you understand what to do, where to do it, when to do it and how often to do it. It is important that you understand the point of the homework, that is, what it is meant to achieve. You and your therapist will usually also discuss any obstacles that may prevent you from carrying out the homework and work at removing them.

In the following session your therapist will ask how you got on with the homework. This is important, and if she or he forgets to check up, you would be wise to bring it up. Therapists are only human so, if they forget, you should remind them.

Similarly, you are only human and sometimes you may not have done your homework. If this happens your therapist will discuss it with you without blaming you. It would be bad if you failed to do your homework, but you are not a bad person for failing; you are a fallible human being. It is, however, important to work out why you didn't do it and try to resolve problems or modify the homework so that you can try again.

Chapter 6
When the going gets tough

Insight number 4, in Chapter 2, points out that usually people have had a great deal of practice at thinking irrationally. There is a very good chance that you have practised your irrational thinking repeatedly and consistently. You are probably an expert at thinking irrationally by now.

The person who developed rational emotive behaviour therapy (REBT), Dr Albert Ellis, realised very early in the day that most people have difficulty in changing long established habits. After more than 50 years' experience in helping people change, he is widely acknowledged as one of the foremost experts in the field of psychotherapy.

When he developed REBT he took into account the fact that people have difficulty changing. Since the start of REBT as a psychotherapeutic approach, many people have developed and refined it. It is now probably one of the most powerful methods of change that you can use when the going gets tough.

Dr Ellis wrote about the issue of 'force and energy' in making changes. Usually when people think about force and energy in making changes they think about some mystical force or some higher power that will make their lives wonderful if only they can somehow tap into it.

This way of thinking is very unfortunate because it encourages people to sit passively and wait until the special force gets around to helping them. Alternatively, they place all their hopes and efforts into some kind of highly improbable event of great good luck, such as winning thousands of pounds in some competition or other.

REBT takes a different view of force and energy. Assuming that certain ideas or beliefs help people to make changes and get rid of psychological disturbances, it is important for the person to practise these helpful ideas in a vigorous, forceful and dramatic way. This is certainly something your therapist will want to help you to do.

Comparing intellectual and emotional insight

Many psychologists and psychotherapists have noted the difference between intellectual and emotional insight. When people are aware of their problems and understand the causes, they are likely to make changes, but not very powerful or lasting changes. When they have emotional insight into these problems they usually make more meaningful and permanent changes.

Dr Ellis suggests that emotional insight has the following characteristics:

1. The person has intellectual insight in that she acknowledges that she has an emotional problem and that her behaviour is self-defeating. Without this step she is unlikely to make progress.
2. The person recognises that her present actions and feelings do not just spring out of the wide blue yonder. The problem does not just 'happen', it has been happening for a while and it happens in certain situations, that is, it had some activating events.

Your therapist will help you to practise recognising these activating events.

3. The person accepts some responsibility for the problem and realises that she has something to do with setting it off in the first place and carrying it on. In terms of the ABC model described in Chapter 3 the person realises that A (the event) does not cause C (the emotional and behavioural consequences). It is primarily B (the person's own beliefs) that determines the feelings and behaviour, and the person is responsible for what she believes. The beliefs are not put there by anyone or anything other than the person herself.
4. The person realises that even if she were encouraged, by having a particularly troublesome childhood, to have some irrational beliefs and to develop painful emotions because of them, that would not essentially be the problem. The problem is that she holds on to the irrational beliefs in the present by practising them and consequently repeatedly 'brain-washing' herself.
5. The person understands she can do something to change her irrational beliefs and, therefore, to change the disturbed feelings of self-defeating actions. The person believes that she can change quite firmly and only occasionally, and weakly, tells herself that she cannot change.
6. The person is determined to work hard at changing her irrational beliefs – to show herself that the irrational beliefs are not true and that they do not fit with reality; to see that the beliefs are contradictory and bring her very poor results; to work hard to give them up and not to go back to believing them again.

Working at changing the beliefs includes the following:

(a) Forcefully and frequently disputing the irrational beliefs as discussed in Chapter 5.

(b) Forcing yourself to go through the difficult and often frustrating process of steadily and repeatedly contradicting the irrational beliefs.

(c) Practising and reminding yourself about the difference between healthy bad feelings, on the one hand, and unhealthy disturbed feeling, on the other, and reminding yourself about the benefits of making changes.

(d) Directly and strongly acting, that is, actually behaving against the irrational beliefs and against the self-defeating actions that they lead to. For example, while working hard to think rationally about panic attacks, repeatedly visiting places where you have panic attacks. Or, while working hard to think rationally about making friends and talking to people, force yourself to go to as many social gatherings as possible.

7. You not only feel determined to work hard at challenging your irrational beliefs, but instead of just thinking about it you actually do work hard at doing this, and do so regularly and strongly.

8. You acknowledge that your disturbed feelings are under your own control and that you can choose to think and act your way out of the disturbed feelings. This means keeping up your determination to work hard and continuously, with action if a new disturbed feeling arises; and dealing with it as quickly as possible.

This involves becoming convinced of some important general rational beliefs, including the following:

> There are no musts in the universe, only preferences.
> Nothing is awful or terrible although many things are bad.
> I can always accept myself no matter what faults I have.
> Although life has many frustrations they are bearable.
> All human beings, including me, are fallible and keep on making mistakes; this is a nuisance but it is not the end of the world.

Finally, the person steadfastly recognises that it is most unlikely that there is any magical solution to her problems and that it is improbable that anyone else will or can remove her troubles for her. Therefore, she had better keep working hard at practising removing those troubles for herself.

Your therapist will help you with all these points. In summary, people who have intellectual insight understand how they create their own problems and what they can do to get rid of them, but they tend only to see things lightly, occasionally and weakly. People who have emotional insight see these things powerfully, often and strongly, and they act upon them. People with emotional insight work hard, often and with vigour, at recognising their irrational beliefs and acting against them, whereas people with intellectual insight do this kind of work mildly, infrequently and weakly.

Your therapist will show you how to work, often strongly and power-fully, against your irrational beliefs in thought and in action. Cognitive therapists in general, and rational emotive behaviour therapists in particular, believe that emotional insight, backed up by consistent hard work at making changes, is the best way to progress.

If you practise disputing and acting against your irrational beliefs, not only will this approach get rid of existing problems it will reduce the likelihood that you will develop new problems in the future. In a sense, it's like giving yourself a 'mental health' inoculation. By practising the ideas in your therapy you give yourself a better chance of dealing effec-tively with the new problems and difficulties that often crop up in the course of people's lives.

Putting force and energy into practice

Take an example of a very typical irrational belief that leads to a great deal of anxiety and depression:

iB: 'I must do well at this task and I have to be liked by other people doing it as well. If I fail it's awful, I can't stand it and it proves I'm no good.'

How can you forcefully work against this belief?

Once again, Dr Ellis offers a number of valuable ideas:

1. You are advised frequently to dispute actively and strongly the irra-tional belief. To do this, you would challenge and question the belief as described in Chapter 5.

The main point is to gain emotional rather than intellectual insight into the irrationality of the belief, and to practise the rational belief more frequently and consistently than you have done previously. Even when you believe the irrational belief you do not believe it 100% of the time. The harder you practise the less you will believe this nonsense, and certainly less often than you do now.

2. Practise the rational belief frequently to acquire the belief that you do not have to succeed and you do not need to have other people's approval, and that you can accept yourself as an imperfect person if you do badly.

Being human, you rarely believe anything completely; you have conflicting views about things. It is typical for a person to believe both the irrational belief and the rational belief at the same time.

In the early stages of change you probably believe the irrational belief strongly most of the time, and the rational belief weakly some of the time. With hard work and practice disputing the irrational belief and practising the rational belief, you will weaken your conviction in the former and strengthen your conviction in the latter.

3. It is important to believe the rational belief more strongly than the irrational belief. It is OK to believe weakly some of the time 'I must do well', as long as you believe strongly most of the time 'I don't have to do well but it would be nice'.

You will tend to act on the belief that you believe most strongly; similarly, the strongest belief would determine the kind of emotions that you feel. Rationally, you hold a strong belief because all the evidence you have seems to support it; irrationally you hold a strong belief because, in spite of the fact that there is no evidence for it, you 'feel' that it is true. In either case you tend to feel and act according to the strongly held belief.

One of the most powerful ways of weakening the irrational belief and strengthening the rational one is the process of disputing described in Chapter 5.

4. Realise that having a belief will not make you act on it; it is important to be determined to think, feel and act against an irrational belief. For example, you could talk very forcefully to yourself: 'I am completely determined to accept myself even if I make mistakes and even if other people disapprove of my mistakes. I can be happy even if they think I am no good'.
5. Push yourself into actions that contradict your irrational belief; this is a powerful way to weaken the irrational belief and reinforce or strengthen your tendency to keep your thinking rational, for example, risk failing at important tasks rather than avoiding them; deliberately make mistakes such as spilling drinks in a pub, to show yourself that it is not awful; to tell people about your weaknesses so as to risk their disapproval.
6. Expect that change will usually require a lot of consistent hard work and practice to make yourself believe healthy ideas. It will probably be wise to keep up the practice for the rest of your life so that you keep on believing healthy ideas.

Even with lots of consistent practice accept the fact that neither you nor anyone else has to be perfectly rational; expect to have setbacks and failures and do not tell yourself that you are no fool for falling back. No matter how many times you fall backwards into irrational thinking, self-defeating actions and disturbed feelings, you can give them up again and return to more healthy habits.

Troubleshooting obstacles and lack of progress

Sometimes people fail to make any progress with their efforts at making changes. This failure was discovered in the earliest stages of psychotherapy in the 1880s and has been the subject of a great deal of study.

Failure to progress is called 'resistance to change' and usually takes place right at the start of the person's efforts or, alternatively, about half-way through. This section of the chapter will help you to understand a bit more about 'resistance' and show you how to do something about it. It is very common to come up against resistance and find that progress seems difficult.

Your therapist understands these difficulties and will work with you to help you overcome them.

Dr Ellis notes that both rational emotive behaviour therapists and cognitive behaviour therapists understand resistance largely in terms of the person's thinking. When the person gets stuck and does not progress it is largely because of his explicit and implicit irrational beliefs. Sometimes irrational beliefs have been so heavily and repeatedly practised that they have become implicit or automatic, such that the person is not immediately aware of holding the beliefs.

Many, perhaps most, of the beliefs that produce resistance are implicit or automatic, that is, it is often difficult to change them without some outside help. These beliefs are difficult to change because, by definition, they are so heavily practised and held with extreme vigour. Therefore, in uprooting them the force and energy described earlier in this chapter is especially important.

Common types of resistance

The most common form of resistance stems from low frustration tolerance. This book has described this important issue to some extent, but a book all about low frustration tolerance, called *Beating the Comfort Trap* by Dr Windy Dryden and Jack Gordon (1993), is a very useful one to read.

Low frustration tolerance centres around short-range hedonism – that is, the person's irrational, dogmatic, short-sighted demands that he receive pleasure immediately or in the short term, even though it will defeat his long-term goals or desires.

The main irrational beliefs associated with low frustration tolerance are: 'I must not be frustrated; I can't stand frustration.' With this belief, when faced with frustration your first thought is to get rid of it as quickly as possible even if, in doing so, you increase your frustration in the long run.

A typical belief of this kind, which can produce resistance, is: 'It should be easy for me to change. I shouldn't have to work hard at it; I can't stand it if it's not easy. It's absolutely awful to have to work hard at changing.'

A second type of belief is: 'I have to be comfortable now, so if changing is uncomfortable I won't do it; I can't stand feeling uncomfortable.' If you hold this belief, once you are comfortable you would fight very hard to avoid discomfort, even if the discomfort would be helpful in the long run.

A third low frustration tolerance belief is: 'I must not experience negative feelings; negative feelings are unbearable.' If you hold on to this belief you will be likely to avoid any situation in which you might have negative feelings. This is especially common in cases where people feel anxious. A belief of this kind would be likely to prevent the person following up disputing with action.

For instance, you may rationally believe 'I do not have to be liked by people but it would be nice', but still avoid going to social gatherings or speaking up because doing so would, at first, be likely to result in feeling anxious. This is so bad because you believe, 'I must not be anxious; I can't stand feeling anxious'.

Indeed this belief is the main cause of 'fear of fear' or, as described earlier in Chapter 3, secondary anxiety.

A final low frustration tolerance belief is: 'I must have good feelings; it would be awful if I didn't and life would be unbearable if I weren't constantly happy.' If you hold on to this belief your life would be characterised by self-defeating actions such as addiction. This belief is a common cause of resistance for people who experience problems with eating, because they believe that they absolutely must have the pleasure that they get from eating something.

If you are stuck and not making the changes you want, one of the things your therapist will want to look at with you is your low frustration tolerance (LFT). LFT is a major reason for lack of change and usually is a very important part of therapy.

Another form of resistance comes from fear of owning up to thoughts, feelings and actions that you regard as shameful. People who experience this kind of problem are usually holding the irrational belief: 'I absolutely should not think, feel or act this way, and I am a terrible person for doing so and deserve to suffer.'

Once again, dispute this forcefully, but especially go back and look at the section on self-downing in Chapter 5. In addition, you might want to read Professor Dryden's book, *Overcoming Guilt* (1994), or Dr Hauck's *Hold Your Head Up High* (1991).

Therapists are used to hearing about things that people consider shameful; do discuss such matters with your therapist who, you will find, understands and is keen to help.

A form of resistance that sometimes occurs early in the process of making changes is caused by the person strongly believing that he is unable to change – that he is hopeless and that change is impossible.

Alternatively, resistance may arise after the person has made some progress and then falls back because he believes: 'My falling back proved it's hopeless and I'll never get better and I am useless. If I was any good at all I should be able to make perfect progress and never have any setbacks.'

If you think this way dispute this irrational belief strongly and vigorously using the ideas in Chapter 5 and this chapter. You might also find it useful to read Dr Hauck's book *Depression* (1974).

An important form of resistance stems from a fear of change or a fear of the future. Many people convince themselves that they: 'absolutely need certainty; without complete certainty life is terribly dangerous and unbearable.'

This irrational belief produces strong feelings of discomfort whenever the person faces uncertainty, and as making changes in your life involves a degree of uncertainty it can cause resistance to change.

The person sticks with the tried and tested even though that brings very unhelpful and undesirable results. Equally important, he protects himself from failure: if you never ask anyone out you never have to face rejection. Of course, you probably have very few friends and spend a lot of time alone, but at least you are not rejected and the possibility of being turned down is too awful even to think about so you only ask someone out if you know for sure that he or she will say yes!

Some people say that a fear of success is a cause of resistance to change, but usually it is not a fear of success but a fear of trying and failing. If we try hard at something and fail, we may lose approval from important people, experience teasing or ridicule, and risk failing at other things. If we try and succeed, we may be faced with new responsibilities that we did not have before and, of course, we may fail at these new responsibilities. Thus making changes is sometimes resisted because of the irrational beliefs about responsibility, failure and certainty.

Irrational beliefs associated with feelings of anger can also result in resistance to change, especially if the irrational belief concerns an intrusion into personal freedom: 'Damn it, I should not have to change; they should change, not me' or 'I should have complete freedom to do anything I want to, even if my actions and feelings are self-defeating'. Beliefs such as this had better be disputed as energetically as possible, but also you may find Dr Hauck's book, *Calm Down* (1980), useful.

Finally, resistance can be caused by 'secondary gain'. There are many situations in which problems and symptoms, although painful, also help us to avoid certain things. One of the main things that people avoid by their difficulties is responsibility and the possibility of failure.

In addition to this, people may hold the irrational belief: 'I am not strong enough to take care of myself; I need someone more able to look after me. I should not have to be responsible for looking after myself. I am useless on my own and I can't stand responsibility.'

Another kind of 'secondary gain' resistance involves getting back at people and is spurred on by irrational beliefs such as, 'My mother must not try to make me eat things I don't like, and she is a rotten person for trying. I'll fix her by not eating at all'.

Once again, using REBT principles to challenge these beliefs, and the resistance that they cause, can be useful for counteracting resistance of this type. It is often difficult to see the 'secondary gain' that arises from our emotional problems. Work with your therapist, being as honest as you can.

Together, you and your therapist, working as a team, stand a good chance of spotting and dealing with secondary gains if they are a problem.

If you believe any of the irrational beliefs discussed in this section, you are likely to come up against blocks to change. If you do, first accept yourself. You are a human being who has a problem, not a problem that masquerades as a human being. All human beings have problems.

It is possible that genetic engineering might one day produce the perfect human being but we don't plan to hold our breath waiting. Instead of telling yourself what a terrible person you are for not progressing with making changes as quickly and effortlessly as you should, go back to patient, forceful, vigorous disputing of the resistance-producing irrational beliefs.

Be as open and as honest as you can be with your therapist, and together you can uncover the blocks to your progress.

Chapter 7
Some other ways of making changes

Most of the time your therapy will be about making major philosophical changes in your irrational beliefs. This is generally the most powerful way of making effective and long-lasting changes.

However, it is likely that you and your therapist will use other methods to understand more about the activating event (A) and to work out the emotional and behavioural consequences.

In addition, your therapist will probably help you with some other ways of making changes which involve changing the activating event. This chapter describes three such methods that are commonly used in therapy to this end: decision-making, changing inferences and learning assertion skills.

These methods are not usually used instead of changing irrational beliefs, but they are often a useful addition to therapy.

All these methods usually follow on after assessing and disputing irrational beliefs, because it is the irrational beliefs that largely determine your unhealthy emotions and self-defeating behaviours. Unless the irrational beliefs are changed first, any other changes that you make are likely to be somewhat superficial and leave you vulnerable to unhealthy emotions and self-defeating behaviours again in the future. The methods of change discussed in this chapter are best used in conjunction with therapy designed to change irrational beliefs. All the methods discussed here involve changing the A. If they are used in conjunction with making changes in the irrational beliefs they can be very useful. It is quite probable that your therapist will help you look at some of the methods discussed in this chapter in your therapy.

Decision-making

This is a strategy devised initially by D'Zurilla and Nezu, two American psychotherapists. It has a number of steps and each one involves asking yourself some questions. It is probably best to write down your answers to each step on a piece of paper. This is something your therapist will be able to help you with.

Step 1

The first step is to ask yourself: What is the problem?

Here the issue at hand is to define as clearly as possible the problem that you want to deal with. Let's take an example: Jim is unhappy at work.

Step 2

What do I want?

Here the main point is to work out your goal, what you want to get to. Jim has several possible goals:

1. Increase his happiness at work.
2. Find another job.
3. Resign and become unemployed.

There are, of course, many other possible goals.

Here the point is to write down as many goals as possible and then pick the one that seems best.

It is often very helpful to use a technique called 'referenting', which involves writing down all the long-term and short-term advantages and disadvantages of each of the various possibilities, and using this to help you make your choice. For instance, in the above example, suppose Jim decides that resigning has a few short-term advantages but many long-term disadvantages, and rejects it.

Remember Chapter 6, however. If Jim suffers from low frustration tolerance, he might conclude that he: 'absolutely must be happy at work and he can't bear being unhappy.' In this case he would be more likely to resign even though this causes him serious long-term disadvantages.

On the other hand, suppose Jim irrationally believes: 'I must make the right decision. If I make the wrong decision that would be terrible; I couldn't stand it. If my decision proves to be a bad one it would mean I am worthless and I could never be happy again.'

If he believes that nonsense he would probably look at the notes he had made, feel very anxious and conclude that he could not make any decision at all. This shows how important it is to use methods of this kind along with REBT.

Suppose Jim decides that his best option is to look for another job.

Step 3

Having answered the question: 'What do I want?', Jim is now faced with the question: 'What do I do to get it?'

This involves exploring as many options and courses of action as possible. In the case of this particular example he could look for jobs in the same field of work or consider a change of career; he could get an appointment with a careers adviser, explore what local colleges have to offer in training courses and ask his friends what they think he would be suited to.

Suppose, however, that he is a keen fan of fashion magazines and television programmes and the option that appeals to him is a new career as a fashion designer.

Step 4

The question is: What might happen?

Here the issue is to consider all the possible consequences if he were to pursue this course of action. Once again the 'referenting' technique described above could be of use. Suppose some of the consequences are:

1. Happier with new job.
2. Have to retrain at college.
3. Don't know anything about grants for courses.
4. Would probably earn less money for a long time.

Now Jim would be advised to find out more about grants for courses and discuss the likelihood of earning less money with his family.

At this point it would, of course, be quite possible for Jim to start thinking irrationally and therefore put a stop to the process. For example: 'I must not inconvenience my family by earning less money. They will hate me for letting them down. I should just forget all this.'

Step 5

What is my decision?

It is at this point that Jim is faced with making a decision and no amount of irrational thinking will help! If he works hard at keeping his thinking rational his decision may still not be easy, but at least he is more likely to make one.

Step 6

Now do it!

Now Jim, having made his decision, will act on it and do what is necessary to put the decision into practice.

Step 7

This is the final step and involves asking: 'Did it work?', 'Has my decision produced the result I wanted?'.

Obviously, with some decisions it may not be possible to answer these questions for some time, but this evaluation step is still important, and if the answer is 'No, it didn't' then it's back to the drawing board and Step 1.

For people who routinely have problems making decisions or who go through this whole seven-step process time after time and still, repeatedly, end up feeling unhappy or dissatisfied, they would be best advised to look to their irrational beliefs and set about making the kinds of changes described and explained earlier in this book, with the help of their therapist.

Nevertheless, this approach can be very helpful for making many different kinds of decisions about changing actual life circumstances, not just about changing jobs.

Changing inferences

Look again at Chapter 4 and the section called 'More details about the "A"s'. That section is about inferences, that is, your perceptions of things that happen to you. These inferences trigger the irrational belief which then determines the emotional and behavioural consequence, C, and it is very likely that your therapist will spend time helping you to uncover the inferences you make about specific events.

These inferences, or perceptions of events, can be accurate or inaccurate. For instance, in Chapter 4 we described the following examples:

A: **Event**:   My wife came home late.
   Inference: She does not care about our marriage.

Consider that this A triggers the following:

iB: She should not do this to me. She must care about our marriage; she is a terrible person for coming home late

This leads to the C of anger.

The key to psychological well-being is to change the irrational belief, but it is advisable in addition to examine the accuracy of the inference: 'She does not care about our marriage.' The event of her coming home late is a fact and as it has already happened it cannot be changed. The inference, however, that 'She does not care about our marriage because she came home late' is not a fact. It is a guess or hypothesis.

It is important to teach yourself the difference between facts and guesses, or inferences as they are technically called. When you examine your inferences about events or facts, practise trying to work out whether or not your inference is true or false.

In doing this look for two kinds of mistakes that people make:

1. Mistakes in gathering information.
2. Mistakes in drawing conclusions from information

Dr Beck is the pioneer of cognitive therapy and he specialises in helping people to change these kinds of mistakes in their inferences. He suggests that there are two main ways in which people go wrong in gathering information: 'selective abstraction' and 'magnification or minimisation'.

Selective abstraction means focusing on one detail out of context and ignoring other features of the situation. For instance, if you thought to ask your wife why she was late you might learn that she had a flat tyre!

Magnification/minimisation involves making grossly distorted errors in evaluation. For instance, it may be that 99 times in every 100 my wife is not late, but this one time she is proves that she does not love me!

In both these types of error people ignore some features of the situation and concentrate on one or two particular aspects. In other words, they do not get enough information about the situation as a whole; they are biased in the way that they gather information.

Try to practise keeping accurate records of situations without concentrating on one aspect and without blowing one thing out of proportion. Keep your notes as accurate as possible: this is often a common homework assignment in therapy.

It is, of course important to realise that your inference may be accurate in the first place, in which case it is important to work on the irrational belief that it triggered. Indeed, if you work hard at thinking rationally, you make it much more likely that your inferences will be an accurate understanding of the situation.

According to Dr Beck there are, broadly speaking, three types of mistakes made in drawing conclusions from situations. These are: 'arbitrary inferences', 'over-generalisation' and 'personalisation'.

Arbitrary inference involves drawing a conclusion in the absence of supporting evidence or in the face of contradictory evidence: for example, insisting that someone does not love you when he keeps telling you he does.

Over-generalisation involves drawing a general conclusion on the basis of a single incident: for example, because I failed that examination I'm stupid and I'll never pass another examination as long as I live.

Personalisation means relating external events to oneself when there is no basis for making such a connection: for example, when you see a group of people laughing you assume that they are laughing at you.

All of these kinds of mistake in inferences involve drawing inaccurate conclusions from actual events. Try to teach yourself to draw fair and justifiable conclusions from the things that you see going on around you.

Practise by keeping a diary of your conclusions: this is another typical homework assignment. Practise, too, collecting information about events as accurately as possible before you draw conclusions.

Dr Beck advises that people dispute their inferences in a way that is similar to disputing irrational beliefs, that is, by asking themselves questions. He suggests the use of three basic questions:

1. What's the evidence?
2. What is another way of looking at the situation?
3. So what if it happens?

For example, take the inference: 'Because my wife came home late she does not love me.' What evidence proves that she does not love me? What evidence is there to show that this is why she came home late? What evidence suggests that she does, in fact, love me. These questions are intended to help you to determine whether or not you are making any of the mistakes listed above.

Similarly, I could ask myself: 'What is another way of looking at this? Is it possible there is an alternative explanation for her coming home late? Is there any possibility that I am overlooking?'

Finally, one might follow Beck's advice and ask: 'So what if she does come home late? How bad is that? Is it really terrible or is it a nuisance? What is the worst that could happen? How likely is it that the worst thing will happen?'

This latter strategy may help, but unless you also challenge the irrational dogmatic demand as well, it is unlikely to be particularly helpful. Dr Beck points out that mistaken inferences often go hand in hand with irrational beliefs. For example, a person might irrationally believe: 'I absolutely should not have failed that exam, and because I did I am a complete worm.'

He may then create the false inference, 'I know I will never amount to anything'.

The faulty inference is an example of what Ellis calls 'all or none thinking' and what Beck refers to as 'arbitrary inference'. It would be important to dispute both the irrational belief and the faulty inference, but please note that, if the person went on to say, rationally: 'I might want to be successful but I don't absolutely have to be and I can accept myself even if I'm not', the faulty inference per se would not be especially harmful.

That is why extra attention is usually given to the irrational beliefs rather than inferences.

Another example of faulty inferences provided by Dr Beck is that of 'emotional reasoning'. In this case the person asserts 'I am a failure because I feel like a failure'.

Ellis points out that feeling something is true does not make it true. You may 'feel' you are going to win £1000 000 this week, but that feeling does not mean you will actually win anything; similarly, if you feel that the moon is made of green cheese, does that 'feeling' mean that it is made of green cheese.

This inference in itself is not the cause of emotional distress or self-defeating behaviour, because the person might rationally think: 'I am a failure because I feel like a failure, but I do not have to be a success even though it would be nice. I can accept myself as a fallible human being.'

Nevertheless, it is wise to challenge, or dispute, mistaken inferences.

People are likely to be disturbed emotionally and engage in self-defeating actions if they routinely make mistaken inferences, or if they hold on to irrational beliefs. People who hold on to irrational beliefs are more likely to make mistaken inferences than people who hold rational beliefs.

However, it is possible to think rationally but still make mistaken inferences. People who experience the most trouble are those who think irrationally and make mistaken inferences. Therefore, although it is advisable to concentrate most effort on changing the irrational beliefs it is as well to work on changing mistaken inferences too.

Assertion skills

Dr Paul Hauck is an expert in the area of assertion skills and if you would like to read more about this topic than there is space for here, we recommend his book *How to Stand Up for Yourself* (1981).

Dr Hauck states there are three key objectives in having a relationship with anyone, whether the relationship is one of marriage, friendship, employer to employee, or parent to child. We want cooperation, respect and love from each other.

We want cooperation from people who provide us with daily services, such as those who work in shops or on public transport. We do not really want them to respect or love us, but cooperation is important.

We want respect from people with whom we have more involvement, for example, our employers, teachers or bank managers. The level of involvement is more than cooperation and these types of relationships have more far-reaching consequences than the previous ones, and respect usually has to be earned.

Finally, we want love from those to whom we devote our lives and who can help us satisfy important desires; this includes our spouse, family and closest friends.

Although fundamentally we do create our own emotional problems, we also play an indirect role in the creation of emotional problems in other people.

We are often puzzled by the unfair treatment we receive at the hands of loved ones, friends or work mates, and spend hours trying to work out why they do this to us. There are many possible reasons (maybe they don't care, maybe they do it by mistake, maybe they are ignorant of the consequences of their actions to us) but the key point is not why they do it but how we can get them to change.

Dr Hauck suggests that there are two principles of human reaction:

1. We get the behaviour we put up with.
2. If we want to change someone else's behaviour we had better change our own first.

Behaviour exists because it is reinforced as B.F. Skinner, a famous psychologist, demonstrated. Children are lazy around the house because their parents tolerate it and colleagues at work push an extra load on to us because we let them.

If you are involved in a close relationship of the kind where respect and/or love are important, and you are not being treated as you would like to be, you are somehow reinforcing the behaviour that you dislike. If you want the other person to change you will first have to change yourself. If you are not reinforcing the behaviour then someone else is.

For example, it could be that your spouse's undesirable actions are being reinforced by your parents-in-law, or your work mates' actions by other colleagues, but someone, if not you, is reinforcing it.

You are not responsible for the other person's behaviour but you are inadvertently reinforcing it by maintaining a situation in which the behaviour can be fostered and keep on happening.

Reinforcement means that, if behaviour is rewarded or encouraged in some way, it will be strengthened and become more likely to keep happening. If it is not rewarded it tends to be extinguished. However, behaviour that is sometimes rewarded and sometimes not tends to be powerfully reinforced. Therefore, it is important to be consistent and not lapse into occasional reinforcement.

Before deciding whether or not to act assertively it is very important to look at your irrational beliefs about the behaviour that you dislike and the person or people who are responsible for it. You will almost certainly act aggressively not assertively, if you are thinking irrationally about these things.

So, before proceeding, work hard to change your irrational beliefs into rational beliefs and allow the disturbed emotions you feel, which will probably be anger, to turn into healthy negative emotion such as annoyance. Then you will be in a position to act assertively.

At that point you still have to decide whether you want to act assertively or not.

Hauck advises that it is wise to do something about our frustrations if we are less than reasonably content for a prolonged period of time. If this happens we will probably recognise psychological and physical symptoms of stress.

Just as we know when we are thirsty or hungry, we know when we are being manipulated, threatened or treated unfairly at a level beyond that which we are willing to put up with. These messages that the body sends us are important. If we ignore them for a long period we are likely to be unhappy and may make ourselves emotionally disturbed.

We will probably also want to end the relationship. When frustrations and/or conflicts are ever present they leave the sufferer feeling unhappy, tired and low in energy, and increase the chances that they will think irrationally, leading to the disturbed emotions and self-defeating behaviour discussed so far in this book.

If you find yourself in that situation:

1. Work hard at rational thinking.
2. Be assertive with the people who are behaving in ways that you don't like.

What is assertive behaviour?

So what is assertion? Assertion is the appropriate expression of feelings and desires. A person who is thinking irrationally is less likely to be able to express her feelings and desires appropriately. Instead, she is more likely to give in to others too quickly, or to be aggressive and argumentative.

Hence the importance of working on irrational thinking first.

Two important 'words of warning' are:

1. Behaving assertively is no guarantee that you will get what you want, though it may well increase the likelihood of a favourable outcome.
2. Even if you can be assertive you do not have to be so all the time; it is important to assess the consequences of your assertiveness first. It is, for example, not always helpful to be assertive with your boss, especially when he or she is feeling angry.

Assertive behaviour is characterised by a statement of preference or request for someone else to change his actions. It is spoken clearly and directly, but without hostility or blame.

Some guidelines for assertiveness include the following:

1. When refusing a request say 'no' decisively. If you are able, explain why you are refusing but don't be apologetic. If possible offer the person another course of action.
2. If asked to respond to some question or request be as brief as possible without interruption.
3. When asked to do something that is unreasonable ask for an explanation.

4. Look directly at the person and look confident and calm, even if you don't feel that way. Don't shout or speak too softly.

5. When expressing annoyance or criticism, comment on the person's reaction not the person himself, and avoid making a personal attack. Instead of saying, 'Listen, you sod, I hate it when you are inconsiderate', be specific: 'I feel annoyed when you are late for meetings and I'd prefer it if you would come on time or let me know if you will be late.'

6. Keep a record of your assertive responses and reward yourself each time that you are assertive.

7. Don't tell yourself what a worm you are if you fail to act assertively. Accept yourself for your faults and try to act better next time.

Three rules of assertiveness

Hauck suggests three rules of assertion.

First rule

If someone does something good for you express your gratitude and try to do something good for him or her. This is a fundamental rule and, if people follow it, it usually prevents problems arising in the first place. You may also try doing something good for someone before they do something good for you and see what happens!

It is important to develop a healthy trusting attitude towards other people and to have confidence that they will probably not take advantage of you. With this attitude as a starting point you can then begin to discriminate, on the basis of experience, between people whom it is wise to trust and people whom it is not.

Second rule

If people do something bad to you and they don't realise that they are behaving badly, it is wise to turn the other cheek, forgive them, while working hard to avoid making yourselves angry. Assertively point out to them your feelings and desires.

If that does not work try to keep away from them, but if you cannot keep away realise that you may be reinforcing their behaviour. Therefore, if you lecture them and whinge and moan but keep on otherwise acting as you were, their behaviour is likely to continue.

It is most important that you do not make irrational demands that they change, do not get angry, and do not insist irrationally that they are terrible, worthless nothings for acting this way. Instead, work hard to stick with your healthy preference and work hard to remind yourself that it is their behaviour that is bad not them as people.

If they will not be reasoned with you had better show them by your actions that they do have every right to continue behaving badly, but if they do you will not tolerate their behaviour.

Third rule

According to Hauck the third rule is that, when all else has failed, if someone continues to behave badly and you cannot keep out of his way because, for example, you live with him, do something equally bad to him.

For instance, if your children absolutely refuse to tidy their room and leave it in a constant mess and will not listen to reason, you might show them that you, too, can behave unreasonably by refusing to wash their clothes until they mend their ways.

If colleagues at work continue to pile their work your way in an unreasonable fashion and refuse to listen to reason, complain to your boss or to your union representative: do not simply suffer in silence.

In the short run, if you get this far you have probably taught people to treat you badly and you will now surprise them by suddenly changing your behaviour, because they will not be expecting this. Consequently, their behaviour will probably get worse for a while before it gets better.

In the long run your aim is to teach them that their behaviour will not be tolerated and will not produce good results for them. It is very important that you engage in an assertive behaviour without anger or aggression on your part.

Finally, of course, sometimes people simply will not modify their behaviour no matter what you do. If that proves to be the case it is important that you follow the advice set out in this book and work hard at thinking rationally about the difficult situation that you are in. Thinking irrationally will make a difficult situation ten time worse. If you work at thinking rationally you still have options.

First option

Put up with the situation. If the situation or the person provides you with other things that you consider worth having, you can choose to tolerate the bad in order to get the good.

Second option

Leave the situation. A bad job or an abusive relationship does not have to be forever. If the relationship provides you with nothing of value and many things that are physically or emotionally painful, then take steps to leave.

It may, for example, be difficult to think rationally if you have faced months or years of abuse from your spouse, but nevertheless it is important to try. When you begin to think rationally about yourself, your partner and your relationship together, even in that difficult situation, we think that you will see that your do not have to live in a violent relationship.

You can make it on your own.

Chapter 8
Conclusion

This book has described the process that people experience when they go though rational emotive behaviour therapy (REBT). REBT is a powerful form of psychological therapy which has been used by many thousands of people to change their lives for the better. This book is intended for you to read in conjunction with actual therapy.

You can of course learn lots of things from books, but there is no real substitute for actual therapy. This book may be helpful if you are considering getting therapy for help with your problems.

You and your therapist form a team with the task of working together to help you to make changes. The therapy is based on mutual respect, with each member of the team being equally important. Your therapist is an expert in making changes and can advise you how to go about making the changes you want.

What are the main conclusions to be drawn from this book?

1. It is healthy to accept that you are responsible for how you feel, what you think or believe, and what you do. No matter how much other people may try to provoke you into feeling or doing certain things, you ultimately get yourself worked up by your habits of thinking, that is, by your irrational beliefs.
2. All people have a strong tendency to think irrationally; your emotional and behavioural problems are not the fault of your childhood or your parents; they are determined mainly by your irrational thinking. Of course this is not to say that it is good to have had an unhappy childhood, but you are likely to have been working hard on your irrational thinking for a long time.
3. Your irrational beliefs are probably long held and firmly practised, so they will take hard work to change.
4. Accept yourself 'warts and all'. All of us are imperfect humans prone to making mistakes, but fortunately for us we do not have to be perfect.

5. Work hard against a dogmatic 'must be' philosophy and practise developing a non-demanding and flexible way of looking at and interacting with yourself, with other people and the world in general.

6. It is mentally healthy to acknowledge reality; you cannot change reality merely by thinking, so your demand that it should not be as it is will accomplish nothing except your own happiness. Having accepted reality do your best to act in ways that can change things for the better.

7. When you can't change things, or when things change only very slowly, develop a healthy ability to tolerate or withstand frustration and while doing so gain enjoyment from other aspects of your life. Teach yourself, and continually remind yourself, that experiencing healthy negative emotions is realistic and beneficial when you face negative life events. You do not have to eradicate every hint of emotional discomfort from your life.

8. Develop and spend time engaged in hobbies, pleasure pursuits and special projects that engage your interests and are important to you. Set aside time regularly for yourself for this purpose; this is not selfishness, it is healthy enlightened self-interest.

9. Work hard on relationships with other people by accepting people for their richness and diversity. Accept people as people who are fallible and do not have to be perfect, although this does not mean that you should tolerate or accept bad behaviour. If people behave badly, do not accept their bad behaviour but remind yourself that it is the behaviour that is bad not the person. Practise communicating your positive and negative feelings to other people, work hard to keep your promises but accept yourself as fallible if you do let someone down. Treat other people as you would like them to treat you.

10. Accept that as you are a normal human being you will probably never be completely mentally healthy and free of problems and frustrations. Therefore, practise a healthy attitude to your own problems. Admit that you have a problem and accept yourself for having it and then work hard at making changes, with your therapist's help.

It is an exciting and rewarding journey.
Bon voyage!

Bibliography

Dryden W (1994) *Overcoming Guilt*. London: Sheldon Press.

Dryden W, Gordon J (1990) *Think Your Way to Happiness*. London: Sheldon Press.

Dryden W, Gordon J (1991) *How to Untangle Your Emotional Knots*. London: Sheldon Press.

Dryden W, Gordon J (1993) *Beating the Comfort Trap*. London: Sheldon Press.

Hauck P (1974) *Depression*. London: Sheldon Press.

Hauck P (1980) *Calm Down*. London: Sheldon Press.

Hauck P (1981) *How to Stand up for Yourself*. London: Sheldon Press.

Hauck P (1991) *Hold Your Head up High*. London: Sheldon Press.

Walen S, DiGuiseppe R, Dryden W (1992) *A Practitioner's Guide to Rational–Emotive Therapy*. New York: Oxford University Press.

Index